Performing the Word

PERFORMING THE WORD

Fahamisha Patricia Brown

African American Poetry as Vernacular Culture

RUTGERS UNIVERSITY PRESS
New Brunswick, New Jersey, and London

Library of Congress Cataloging-in-Publication Data
Brown, Fahamisha Patricia, 1942–
    Performing the word : African-American poetry as vernacular
culture / Fahamisha Patricia Brown.
      p.   cm.
    Includes bibliographical references and index.
    ISBN 0-8135-2631-0 (alk. paper). — ISBN 0-8135-2632-9 (pbk. :
alk. paper)
    1. American poetry—Afro-American authors—History and criticism.
2. Afro-American oral tradition—United States. 3. Afro-Americans
in the performing arts. 4. Language and culture—United States.
5. Afro-Americans in literature. 6. Afro-Americans—Civilization.
7. Black English. I. Title.
PS310.N4B76   1999
    811.009'896073—dc21
98-46273

British Cataloging-in-Publication data for this book is available from the British Library

Manufactured in the United States of America

Design by John Romer

Dedication

For my mother, Anna Mae Martin Brown
my grandmother, Lula Bowman
my great-aunt, Irene Bell
my great-grandmother, Mary Wenn Brown

Contents

Acknowledgments

When a book is thirty years in the making, credit for its ultimate form goes to many people: First, to the students who sat in my classrooms while I tried out these ideas at Malcolm X Community College, the University of Massachusetts at Boston, Boston State College, Tufts University, Boston College, Trinity College, and Fordham University; to Moses E. Wilson Jr. and family, who gave me a home and the use of a computer so I could complete this manuscript; to Trinity College, Fordham University, and the Schomburg Center for Research in Black Culture, all of which gave me time and space to read, think, and write; to my dissertation committee, Robert Kern, Suzanne Matson, and especially Carol Hurd Green, who helped me through the new chapter; to Mark Naison who steered me to a publisher; to Gloria Hull and the other participants in the Yale/MLA summer seminar of 1977; to Charla Mae Rollins, the librarian who gave me a copy of the Arna Bontemps poetry anthology *Golden Slippers* and started my lifelong love affair with African American poetry; and most especially to the poets, those I've known in person and those I've known only through the pages of a book, a reading, or a recording. All of you have made this book possible.

Performing the Word

Toward a Vernacular Theory of African American Poetry

"If you can say it, you can play it," a drummer friend of mine used to say to his students. His lessons to his drummers and the dancers they accompanied expressed the relationship between sound and rhythm and the ways in which the two combine to create meaning. These relationships are a key element in African and African diaspora cultures.[1] This study explores the written manifestations of that cultural expression, specifically in poetry written by African Americans. I situate African American poetry in African American vernacular expressive culture, its language practices and performativity. By doing so, I hope to offer readers, teachers, and students of African American poetry a way of reading, understanding, and appreciating a body of work that has received little critical attention. Although African American literary tradition begins with the eighteenth-century poets Lucy Terry, Jupiter Hammon, and Phillis Wheatley, a search for critical discussions of African American poetry reveals sparse treatment compared to that for prose narrative. Studies of American poetry, whether theoretical or critical, rarely draw their examples from among the works of African American poets. Aside from a few studies of "major" poets, such as Langston Hughes, Gwendolyn Brooks, Robert Hayden, and Rita Dove, or period histories of such phenomena as the Harlem Renaissance or the New Black Arts movement, there has been little sustained critical inquiry into African American poetry as a body of literature. This work represents such an inquiry.

African American poetry is, of course, a part of the larger Anglo-

American poetic tradition, and its earliest practitioners had as one of their goals the demonstration of the literary capabilities of the race. However, African Americans have always existed as much apart from as a part of the society and culture of the United States of America. *De jure* and *de facto* segregation have insured that there remains a distinctively African American modality of cultural expression within the larger American context (although, at its edges, distinctively African American blurs into the American and vice versa). I situate my discussion of African American poetry in African American vernacular cultural expression. In my study, I use the term *vernacular culture* to refer to the expressive culture of people descended from Africans enslaved in that part of North America that became the United States of America. Their culture was an invention, or reinvention, forged out of historical, sociopolitical, and cultural necessities. Africans from many linguistic and cultural backgrounds became one people separated from the larger community of "Americans." African American cultural expression, including literature, also evolved separate from the mainstream of American cultural expression, even as African Americans strived to demonstrate literary competence within that mainstream.

Critics position poetry by African Americans within the English language or American literary scene and evaluate it as good, bad, or mediocre by whatever the prevailing critical standard of the day happens to be. Most often, the critical judgment is that poetry by African Americans is, for the most part, lacking in literary merit or an inadequate imitation of its white models.[2] Most of the early commentary makes the assumption that African American poetry should be studied and criticized as poetry in the English language. Yet aside from William Stanley Braithwaite's early-twentieth-century anthologies of magazine verse and James Weldon Johnson's anthology of American Negro poetry, published in the period between the two World Wars, works by African American poets rarely were included in studies or anthologies of American poetry. Johnson's anthology began a tradition of separate anthologies for poets of African descent. The prefaces to the two editions of Johnson's anthology mark the beginning of a critical tradition for this body of work. For reasons beyond the scope of this study, the consignment of works by African American poets almost exclusively to anthologies and studies of African American poetry—also identified as Negro, Black, or Afro-American—with an almost total exclusion of their work from studies of American poetry[3] has continued, leaving this body of work largely unexamined. Given such de facto segregation of texts, it seems appropriate to examine such texts where they are, as an identifiable and distinct tradition within the broader traditions of American and English-language poetry.

In *Black Atlantic,* Paul Gilroy explores the ways that critics use the concept of a cultural tradition. "The idea of tradition gets understandably invoked to underscore the historical continuities, subcultural conversations, intertextual and intercultural cross-fertilisations which make the notion of a distinctive and self-conscious black culture appear plausible" (190). It is in the "subcultural conversations" and "intertextual cross-fertilisations" that Amiri Baraka's concept of "the changing same"[4] becomes apparent. African American poetic texts are in conversation with African American vernacular cultural texts as well as with each other and the larger body of English-language texts. "Like ethnicity, a racial tradition usually connotes a self-perceived group of people who hold in common a set of . . . traditions and folkways not [necessarily] shared by the other people with whom they are in constant contact and interaction" (Hogue, *Race* 5). Thus, although I concede an essential hybridity of African American culture, in this work I explore the specificity of that culture.

In what lies the "Blackness" of African American and other "Black" poetries? What elements in the poetry constitute Henry Louis Gates's "Black Difference"?[5] This study examines elements of African American expressive culture—its language practices, both folk and popular, that is to say both the rural and peasant as well as the urban and contemporary. Recognizing with W. Lawrence Hogue that "all literary theories imply a particular form of politics or presuppose a certain use of literature" (*Discourse* 14), in my study I use aspects of various critical approaches. From the new historical to the postmodern and poststructural, from reader response to cultural studies, not to mention the New Criticism, which informed my earliest literary studies, I have gleaned whatever is useful for my purposes. Each theoretical approach plays some part in the way I read the work of African American poets. For "a literary text's value and worth are determined within a cultural context" (Hogue, *Discourse* 15). "A little bit of this and a little bit of that," according to my great-grandmother, "will flavor the dish up right." My context is African American vernacular culture. I hope the seasoning clarifies my argument.

I configure the traditionally defined poetic genres of lyric, narrative, and drama in African American vernacular terms as song/talk, story, and voicings. I also explore the primacy of the sermonic mode or, to use a term coined by Gwendolyn Brooks, preachment[5] in African American poetic tradition. Why does so much of the poetry contain sociopolitical comment? Additionally, I explore the nature of textual performativity. In what way do these texts speak to their readers and engender dialogue or conversation? Like poetry in general, African American poetry has its roots in song and the spoken word. Expressed in the language of the people, heightened to express feelings or thoughts outside the range of everyday conversation, this poetry evokes immediate complex responses that can be enhanced through reflection. It can be heard and responded to immediately, and it can be contemplated at leisure.

When I speak of African American vernacular poetry, then, I am speaking of a very broad tradition of language practice. Stephen Henderson, in his seminal 1973 study of African American poetry, and Gordon Rohlehr, in his 1989 discussion of Caribbean poetry in English, offer us a way of describing such a tradition. Each identifies a "continuum" of language practice among the speakers and writers of English. African American poets have at their disposal a language continuum ranging from a communally based vernacular, what I call the mother tongue, to the academic or literary language learned in schools. Just as I use a different register of language with my family and circle of intimates than with my professional colleagues or in my classrooms, so the poet, too, uses varied registers of language depending on the situation or world of the poem.

African American vernacular practice can be plain or fancy depending upon the audience and situation. Urban argot and rural dialect are not the only registers of Blackness. As Sonia Sanchez points out in an interview with Derrick Gilbert (a.k.a. D-Knowledge), "as an African-American and as an African, you can take anything and do with it what you want to do. . . . We are connected to a tradition of writing that people came to through learning on their own" (Gilbert 223). It is this African American tradition of writing that my work explores. Although I organize my discussion in part based on the publication dates of anthologies of African American poetry, for the most part I do not depend upon such a strict chronology. Mine is an exploration of a "changing same," a study of a tradition. I am examining the ways in which African American poets participate in, extend, and revise vernacular practice.

What my study assumes, but does not discuss at any length, is the hybrid nature of African American culture, including its literature. African American poetry is, after all, American. Just as there is no such thing as American popular music without its African American presence, so there is no such thing as American literature without its African American presence. To determine, however, whether the African practice of describing through enumeration or listing is more significant in the work of African American poets than is the Whitmanesque practice of enumeration might prove to be an impossibility. To determine whether the Anglo-American folk ballad or the British literary ballad is the more significant influence on the use of the ballad form by African American poets might prove equally difficult. As a former folk singer, I am aware that two "American" folk ballads have African American authors—"The Ballad of Jesse James" by Billy Gashade, who included his name in a signature stanza, and "Casey Jones" by Wallace Saunders, who sold his copyright for a bottle of gin. Still another subject for further exploration is the nature of the frequent use by African American poets of the sonnet form, as in Rita Dove's work *Mother Love.*

A much more comprehensive exploration of sound and rhythm in African American poetry than is found in this study could be made. Aldon Nielsen's *Black Chant* (1997) explores the soundings and graphology of African American poetry in relationship to blues and jazz. Further questions might include the following: How do African American poets manipulate rhyme and meter, particularly in an age of free verse? What is the relationship between scat singing and the poetic uses of "pure sounds" or nonsense syllables? What is the impact of reading poems to musical or percussion accompaniment? What is the relationship between Beat and New Black Arts styles of performance and those of contemporary rap and slam poets?

That a poet like Derek Walcott of St. Lucia is now being included in anthologies of African American literature and poetry puts into discussion the question of what constitutes "Americanness." The presence of Jamaican Claude McKay and Sierra Leonean Gladys Casely-Hayford in the canon provides precedent. An increasing Caribbean presence is visible in African American vernacular culture. Artists born in the United States, both of Caribbean and non-Caribbean origin, affect Caribbean accents in their recordings and performances. Contemporary hiphop and rap owe as much to Black British and Caribbean dub poets as they do to Gil Scott Heron, the New Black Arts poets, and the Last Poets. The late sixties also introduced "Nuyorican" as a cultural concept and "Spanglish" as a language.[6] Ntozake Shange and others use Spanish phrases in their poems without translation, and writers of Latin American origin, such as Victor Hernandez Cruz, freely mix languages in their poems as they claim Spanish, African, and Native American heritage. Paul Gilroy's concept of the Black Atlantic gives us terms in which to engage an increasingly multinational, multiethnic discourse. We remember that Langston Hughes, by translating Leopold Sedar Senghor of Senegal, Leon Damas of Martinique, and Nicolas Guillen of Cuba, introduced other registers of Blackness to a mostly monolingual United States.

Finally, if didacticism is as central as I claim it to be in this work, what is being preached and what is being taught? Are there African American subjects and themes? Do the poets engage "universal" themes in a particular way? Potential answers to such questions would require a shelf of books. "The half ain't been told." And I do not attempt to answer all the questions raised by my approach to the poetry. What I hope to present is a broad sketch of the place of African American poetry in African American vernacular culture. For these poets perform the word on the page and on the stage. We can hear their words silently or out loud.

Mother Tongue

· ·

African American Vernacular
Speech as Poetic Language

CHAPTER 1

Lately
everybody I meet
is a poet.
　　　"Look here"
said the tall delivery man
who is always drunk
　　　"whoever can do better
　　　ought to do it. Me,
　　　I'm 25 years old
　　　and all the white boys
　　　my age
　　　are younger than me."
So saying
he dropped a six pack
turned into most of my cousins
and left.
　　　LUCILLE CLIFTON

Language is fossil poetry.
　　　RALPH WALDO EMERSON

Poetry is oral in its origins, originally composed to be sung or chanted to musical accompaniment. New World peoples of African descent, in the manner of their African forebears, developed a mode of creative verbal expression that was primarily oral. Indeed, in the new nation called the United States of America, it was decreed illegal for the enslaved Africans and their antebellum descendants to be taught to read and write. As the slaves began to acquire English-language proficiency, first a "pidgin" and then a creolized form of English emerged as these enslaved Africans of many languages and cultures invented or reinvented a New World African American language and culture. The oral virtuosity that signaled the mastery of this new language remains a mark of status in the culture.[1]

To the degree that African Americans identify themselves or are identified as a separate and distinct people and culture, African American vernacular language is a cultural marker. "You don't have the characteristic problems of most people of your nationality," commented my college voice and diction coach. "Can't you sound a little blacker?" asked the director of a radio commercial for hair products, in which I had been cast as a teacher. African American vernacular speech, or "Black English," is one of the modern "Englishes" of the world. By many linguistic definitions, it is a language. That is, it has a vocabulary, pronunciation system, and syntax that can be identified and codified (see Dillard; Smitherman, 1975). African American vernacular English is not merely colloquial, slang, or vulgar. It is fluid, adaptable language with its own rhythms and intonation, figures and metaphors, as well as a variety of class and regional variants. Language is one of the means by which individuals claim membership in the tribe. Language is also one of the ways through which individuals express their personalities. African American language acts, events, or situations provide for displays of linguistic virtuosity.[2] At the same time, they are markers of a particular mode of cultural expressivity. In the sacred and secular traditions of African American vernacular cultural expression, we can identify modes of language performance: sermon, testimony, and prayer as performed in the traditional Black Church; public oratory in the spheres of political and social life; children's games and jump-rope rhymes; "playin the dozens"; rappin' and signifyin'; tall tales, including toasts and boasts; and the lyrics of the spirituals, shouts, jubilees, gospel songs, field hollers, work songs, blues, jazz, and popular songs. In form, subject, and theme, all of these elements are present in African American poetry. (Many are explained and discussed later.)

J. L. Dillard, in his pioneering study *Black English* (1973), relates African American English to the pidgin and creole languages that are spoken in Asia, Africa, the Pacific, the Caribbean, and elsewhere. "Recent research presents evidence that the English of most American Blacks retains some features, which are common in both Caribbean and West African varieties of English. . . . Like the West Indian varieties, American Black English can be traced to a creolized version of English spoken by slaves; it probably came from the West Coast of Africa" (6). In her study *Black*

Language and Culture (1975), Geneva Smitherman summarizes the historical development of this language. What the slaves did, she theorizes, was to "attempt to fit the words of the new language [English in this instance] into the basic mold and idiomatic structure of their native language[s]. . . . West African-speaking slaves grafted English words and sounds onto their indigenous grammatical patterns, producing West African Pidgin English. . . . Over the years, this pidgin became more systematic and widespread in use and developed into Creole English. . . . English Creole gradually lost its distinctiveness and began to be leveled out in the direction of mainstream American English" (2).

Hence, African American vernacular speech became the everyday language of African American conversation, of African American language situations. Dillard notes the existence in the early eighteenth century of an African Pidgin English in common usage from the West Coast of Africa through the Caribbean to the English-speaking American mainland.

Bernard Katz, in the introduction to his 1968 collection of mostly late-nineteenth-century essays, *The Social Implications of Early Negro Music in the United States,* notes African American language practice, poetry, and song-making skills from as early as 1774. Cultural observers from the late-eighteenth century to the mid-nineteenth noted the poetry and music making skills of this New World people. Henry Edward Krehbiel (1913), too, noted the power of the lyrics of the songs. It was, however, in the intellectual ferment of the Harlem Renaissance in the 1920s that critics began serious examination of African American literary production. James Weldon Johnson's prefatory "Essay on the Negro's Creative Genius," in his anthology *The Book of American Negro Poetry* (1922), offers one of the earliest critical overviews of African American poetry. Johnson begins his discussion with a mixture of sociopolitical and literary-cultural critical purposes: "The final measure of the greatness of all peoples is the amount and standard of the literature and art that they have produced. The world does not know that a people is great until that people produces great literature and art. No people that has produced great literature and art has ever been looked upon by the world as distinctly inferior" (9). Johnson asserts that the Negro is "creator of the only things artistic that have yet sprung from American soil and been universally acknowledged as distinctive American products" (10). These "things artistic" include the animal tales as collected by Joel Chandler Harris in the Uncle Remus stories; the spirituals or slave songs as popularized by the Fisk Jubilee Singers; the cakewalk, an African American dance form; and ragtime music. In the lengthy discussion of the evolution of African American music that follows, Johnson explores ragtime, blues, and spirituals, and it is here that his theory of African American poetry begins to be articulated.

These folk and popular art forms, says Johnson, should be the poet's inspiration. In a description of blues lyrics, Johnson defines "real poetry" as "that elusive thing which nobody can define and you can only tell it is there when you feel it" (15). He contrasts the secular ragtime, and its intricate rhythmic stuctures, with the sacred spirituals, "a mass of noble music" (17), whose emphasis is on melody. In this analysis Johnson makes a point about hybridity in African American art. Ethnomusicologists usually ascribe rhythmic elements of African American music to Africa and melodic elements to European sources. Johnson goes on to describe how ragtime's rhythms reveal and express "irrepressible buoyancy, a keen response to the sheer joy of living," while the spiritual reveals in its melodies a "sense of beauty and deep religious feeling" that has "transfused" the world's art (18). Both the spiritual and ragtime are examples of Black vernacular cultural expression, the former from the world of the peasant folk and the latter from that of the city dweller, the one from unknown composers and lyricists, the other from acknowledged composers.

Johnson's analysis is instructive both for what it affirms and what it fails to affirm. For James Weldon Johnson, African American folk and popular art form the basis for the creation of serious art, but are not themselves serious art. Using the critical standards of his day—of established cultural arbiters—he cannot affirm African American cultural production on its own terms, even as he acknowledges its merit. Johnson does find early manifestations of "serious" African American art in the work of Paul Laurence Dunbar (1872–1906). In a discussion of Dunbar's poetry, Johnson first raises the issue of poetic language. He praises Dunbar as the "first poet from the Negro race in the United States to show a combined mastery over poetic material and poetic technique to reveal innate literary distinction in what he wrote and to maintain a high level of performance" (34). He also notes that Dunbar was the first "to use [dialect] as a medium for the true interpretation of Negro character and psychology" (35). The concern with cultural authenticity and issues of representation reflected in Johnson's words would dominate African American critical discourse through much of the twentieth century. It was on this basis that he issued his famous edict on poetic uses of dialect. African American poets, he pronounced, who have the advantage of "writing in the world-conquering English language," were attempting to break away from the "limitations on Negro dialect imposed by the fixing effects of long convention . . . [in which] Negro dialect . . . is an instrument with but two full stops, humor and pathos" (40–41). Readers and critics have repeated Johnson's criticism with variations over the decades in the face of African American efforts to replicate African American vernacular speech in poetry.

It is important to note, though, that Johnson was writing during a period of the minstrel tradition of white performers in blackface makeup. These minstrels perpetuated stereotypes of African American ignorance and inferiority through the use of songs, skits, and jokes pronounced in a stage "Negro dialect" that emphasized mispronunciations and improper syntax. In Johnson's view, the baggage of the minstrel tradition with its ridicule of African American language styles and its stereotyping of the speakers of such language could not be transcended through artistic usage. Johnson could not get beyond Dunbar's appropriation and revisions of stage Negro dialect to appreciate fully the artistry of Dunbar's dialect poems. Clearly, though, he makes a distinction between the language of "dialect poetry" and African American vernacular speech.

In the preface to the revised edition of *The Book of American Negro Poetry* (1931), Johnson praises a new kind of language being used by poets such as Langston Hughes and Sterling Brown. Their language is not the "dialect of the comic minstrel tradition" but the "common, racy, living, authentic speech of the Negro in certain phases of real life" (4). Johnson expresses regret that Negro dialect has not been developed by "Aframerican" poets into the "literary medium that Burns made of Scottish dialect" (5). He privileges as "authentic" African American vernacular speech but misses authentic revisions of minstrelsy in the best dialect poetry of Dunbar and others. What is significant, though, is that Johnson affirms the creativity of the African American folk and their vernacular expression, particularly the music, as a source for African American poetry. In his own work, *God's Trombones: Seven Negro Sermons in Verse* (1927), Johnson would attempt to transform an African American language event, the folk sermon, into poetry.

In a study of African American orature,[3] Gerald Haslam points out that the folk preacher in the traditional Black church service constitutes the "New World equivalent of the African 'language event,' a joyous, intense interchange in which language was employed both to elicit the sacred and to offer release and solace to the congregation" (4). In the "seven sermons and a prayer" of *God's Trombones,* Johnson spells his words in "American Standard" English, but his rhythms and figures cry out for a "Black" performance evoking the Sunday morning and revival meeting oral poet, the African American preacher.

Sterling A. Brown, too, in his 1937 study *Negro Poetry and Drama,* holds up the vernacular tradition as the root source for African American poetry. Reviewing the published output of the "conscious literary artist[s]" such as Lucy Terry (1730–1821) and Phillis Wheatley (1753?–1784), and of Alberry Whitman (1851–1902), the most published African American poet before Dunbar, Brown dismisses them as "too self-conscious. . . . For the genuine poetry of the Negro of this period [1746 to 1910], for poetry that still has the power to portray and to move, one must go to the sly and sardonic folk-rhymes and the profoundly revealing spirituals" (13). Brown extols both the sacred and the secular aspects of the vernacular, arguing for a poetry steeped in the life experiences of the slave, one that reflects an attitude toward life or philosophy shaped by those life experiences and couched in a language specific to that community. In his discussion, he describes a syncretic art: a New World people have created a New World art.

However, Brown, like Johnson, also had problems with nineteenth-century poets' rendition of Negro dialect in print. "Many of the authors were preachers and teachers, consciously literary, who looked down with good humored condescension upon a ridiculous way of life, or were shocked by the departures of the folk from gentility. A few pat phrases, a few stock situations and characteristics, some misspellings: these were the chief things necessary. The wit and beauty possible to folk speech, the folk-shrewdness, the humanity, the stoicism . . . they seldom saw" (42). Brown, too, distinguished between the language of "conventionalized dialect poetry" and the vernacular. "Dialect, or the speech of the people, is capable of expressing whatever the people are. . . . Poets more intent upon learning the ways of the folk, their speech, and their character, that is to say better poets, could have smashed the mold" (43). In poems like "Ma Rainey" from his collection *Southern Road* (1932), Sterling Brown met his own challenge.

What these early critics, in their praise of the folk art, rarely discussed was the degree to which early African American poets were intent upon demonstrating their language competency. Paul Laurence Dunbar probably wrote at least one poem in every verse form known in English prosody. African American poets from the late nineteenth century on, but most notably in the twentieth century from Claude McKay to Gwendolyn Brooks to June Jordan to Rita Dove, continue to stretch the limitations of the sonnet's fourteen lines of iambic pentameter. The unstated goal has been the demonstration of African American competence and equality. I would argue that this concern with form and technique is informed by African American vernacular practice. "It ain't what you do, it's the way how you do it."

The onset of the modern age in American letters after World War II saw critical attention focus on African American prose narrative. That the age of Richard Wright, Ralph Ellison, and James Baldwin is also the age of Margaret Walker, Gwendolyn Brooks, Robert Hayden, Margaret Danner, Melvin B. Tolson, and others tends to be overlooked, despite Walker's Yale Younger Poets Award in 1942 and Brooks's Pulitzer Prize in 1950. In 1963, however, Arna Bontemps published his small anthology, *American Negro Poetry* (in what was something of a supplement to the larger anthology he had coedited with Langston Hughes, *The Poetry of the Negro, 1746–1949*). His overview of African American poetry also argued for a vernacular reading of this literature. Comparing the poetry to African American musical forms, he argued that African American poetry was "marked by a certain special riff, an extra glide, a kick where none is expected and a beat for which there is no notation" (xiii). Arguing for a language practice characterized by specific formal and rhythmic effects, Bontemps continued, "It follows the literary traditions of the language it uses [English], but does not hold them sacred" (xiii).

Similarly, Donald B. Gibson, writing at the height of the Black Arts movement, in his introduction to a collection of critical essays, *Modern Black Poets* (1973), discussed African American poetry in terms of cultural specificity. Gibson described African American poetry as "ideological . . . consciously and explicitly didactic . . . highly irreverent toward conventional notions of sex . . . Yet . . . highly moralistic . . . clear, frank, and explicit" (10). In a discussion of African American poetic language, he pointed out its orality and concrete vocabulary yet nuanced nature. "This language [has a] conscious difference from Standard English [in] its renaming of things and events (its recasting of experience into its own terms)" (11). Gibson's description of African American poetic language is significant because it delineates aesthetic assumptions common to the poetic practice of the Black Arts movement of the late 1960s and early 1970s. This "Black Aesthetic" extended some of the critical assumptions of the Harlem Renaissance and early modern writers.

Adherents to a Black Aesthetic called for an "art for people's sake." They saw the poet as a performer in relationship to an audience. "The poet in his reading or performance assumes a role not unlike that of the black preacher, and the audience becomes its congregation" (Gibson, 12). His description might easily be applied to African American poetry as written and performed by such poets as Amiri Baraka, Haki Madhubuti, Nikki Giovanni, Sonia Sanchez, and others. Gibson's description of the poet as "exhorter, the interpreter of things, the namer and definer" (12) points to a public and communal role for the poet. As is discussed later, this social function—for one who engages in what is an essentially solitary act—is a major trait of African American vernacular culture.

Also in 1973, Stephen B. Henderson's *Understanding the New Black Poetry: Black Speech and Black Music as Poetic Reference* was published. This poetry anthology was organized to demonstrate the close relationship between African American poetry and folk and popular musical and oral forms. Henderson's introductory essay, "The Form of Things Unknown," offered the first coherent theory of African American poetry since Sterling Brown's 1937 work. Henderson posits living African American speech as forming "a kind of continuum of Blackness—at one end instantly identifiable in all of its rich tonal and rhythmic variety, at the other *indistinguishable from that of the whites.* . . . a complex and rich and powerful and subtle linguistic heritage whose resources have scarcely been touched" (32–33; emphasis mine). Henderson identifies a continuum of language practice among African Americans that encompasses both Dunbar's dialect poems and his standard American ones. Similarly, in a 1989 essay, Gordon Rohlehr also posits a "continuum" of language practice for Caribbean poetry in English "stretching between Creole and Standard English, from which speakers naturally select registers of the language which are appropriate to particular contexts and situations" (1–2). This bi- or multidialectism of Black speakers of English has been noted by sociolinguists and is an essential element of African American vernacular speech and, by extension, writing.

What all the previously cited critics share is a view of language, particularly African American vernacular, that is not limited to vocabulary, syntax, and pronunciation. It also encompasses figurative uses of the language, rooted in group and individual experiences, as well as in language as spoken or performed. Metaphor and allusion, devices of repetition, and linguistic sound effects—the matter of oral poetry no matter what its cultural origins or specificity—are the materials through which the African American poet voices her or his art, the mother tongue. The literary traditions that the African American poet explores are both oral and written, a cultural reinvention specific to a syncretic culture.

As African American poetry develops, words and phrases enter the common vocabulary in such a way as to fashion a bedrock of poetic allusion. Stephen Henderson labels this phenomenon *mascon,*[4] "a massive concentration of Black experiential energy which powerfully affects the meaning of Black speech" (44). I describe these linguistically and emotively powerful figures as superallusive, containing meaning that expands as African American poetic texts and sayings are in dialogue with each other.

The ways in which African American poets appropriate the Exodus story as related in the King James Version of the Bible offer a good illustration of how mascon functions in African American poetry: "And the LORD said, I have surely seen the affliction of my people which are in Egypt, and have heard their cry. . . . And I have also seen the oppression wherewith the Egyptians oppress them. Come now therefore, and I will send thee unto Pharaoh, that thou mayest bring forth my people the children of Israel out of Egypt." The spiritual "Go Down Moses," or "Let My People Go," retells the story for a community of slaves, extracting its essence.

> Go down, Moses,
> Way down in Egyptland
> Tell Old Pharaoh
> To let my people go

Tradition says that this spiritual was about Harriet Tubman, often referred to as Moses. But in the spiritual, "Moses" becomes a synonym for any liberator; Pharaoh becomes the symbol for the oppressor; and the hortatory takes its place as a dominant mode in African American discourse.

As the song continues, we can perceive an attitude toward language and spoken word themselves:

"Thus saith the Lord,"
bold Moses said,
"Let my people go."

In the sense of a speech act, the word itself has power. The word makes action possible, even necessary. Further, in the spiritual, the chorus changes after its first indirect statement to direct quotation. "Tell Old Pharaoh/To let my people go" becomes "Tell old Pharaoh/ 'Let my people go.'" The choral refrain of "Go down Moses" gathers force through each repetition. Similarly, the responsorial line, "Let my people go," takes on the weight of its multiple voices and voicings. The call-and-response structure of the verses gives the soloist the authority to speak for the group as she or he recounts the inspiring story. There is direct communication between the poet/song leader/author and the poem's/song's audience/chorus.

The centrality of the Exodus story in African American culture resonates in oral tradition and popular culture to the present day. It is a favorite of African American preachers whether purely in the spiritual context or with its sociohistorical overtones. The story of divine intervention on behalf of the powerless retains its relevance and ability to inspire. "Moses" and "Old Pharaoh" are subjects of countless songs, stories, and sermons and are picked up early as subjects of written poetry as well.

Paul Laurence Dunbar and James Weldon Johnson are among the poets who found poetry in the voice of the African American folk preacher taking as his text the Exodus story. Both Dunbar's "An Ante-Bellum Sermon," circa 1895, and Johnson's "Let My People Go," published in 1927 in *God's Trombones,* are written in the voices of preachers. The two poems, however, focus on different aspects of the preacher's art. Dunbar's preacher assumes the Moses role.

We is gathahed hyeah, my brothahs,
 In dis howlin' wildaness,
Fu' to speak some words of comfo't
 To each othah in distress.
An' we chooses fu' ouah subjic'
 Dis—we'll 'splain it by an' by;
"An' de Lawd said, 'Moses, Moses,'
 An' de man said, 'Hyeah am I.'"

The preacher preaches in the communal "we" and announces his memorized text. In the slave community, the preacher was the one most likely to have access to the written word, and, if he himself did not read, usually had committed significant amounts of text to memory by listening to others read. Thus the written source is mingled with the preacher's own oral retelling of the story—his creative reinvention.

> Now ole Pher'oh down in Egypt
> Was de wuss man evah bo'n
> An' he had de Hebrew chillun
> Down dah wukin in his co'n;
> 'Twell de Lawd got tiahed o' his foolin',
> An' sez he: "I'll let him know—
> Look hyeah, Moses, go tell Pher'oh
> Fu' to let dem chillun go."
>
> "An' ef he refuse to do it,
> I will make him rue de houah,
> Fu' I'll empty down on Egypt
> All de vials of my powah."
> Yes he did—an' Pher'oh's ahmy
> Wasn't wuth a ha'f a dime;
> Fu' de Lawd will he'p his chillun,
> You kin trust him evah time.
>
> An' yo' enemies may 'sail you
> In de back an' in de front;
> But de Lawd is all aroun' you
> Fu' to ba' de battle's brunt.
> Dey kin fo'ge yo' chains an' shackles
> F'om de mountains to de sea;
> But de Lawd will sen' some Moses
> Fu' to set his chillun free.

By assuming the voice of the preacher for his antebellum sermon, Dunbar is demonstrating for his reader, through dramatic re-creation, how the slave preacher appropriated scriptural written text to the service of his people. The preacher becomes a "Moses" or deliverer through the transmittal of the word.

Still another African American language practice manifests itself in the indirection of the preacher's discourse. Joyce Ann Joyce has discussed the nature of indirection in African American poetic practice: "The ability to force the reader to see familiar words in a new context and to deduce the poet's meaning from analogy, imagery, symbolism, short lines contrasting with long ones, comparisons and contrast in descriptions" (120), all help the poet "to say this to say that." Dunbar's reference to "chains an' shackles" is clear and personal to a slave, but probably only part of a familiar story to a more distanced observer. Through "oblique, elliptical and encoded words" (Redmond, 31), the preacher directs his message to several audiences at once.

> But fu' fear some one mistakes me
> I will pause right hyeah to say,
> Dat I'm still a-preachin' ancient,
> I ain't talkn' 'bout today.

The preacher is lying, of course. By drawing attention to the metaphorical nature of his sermon, he is attesting to its eternal truth. He continues in the next stanzas:

> An' de love he showed to Isrul
>   Wasn't all on Isrul spent;
> Now don't run an' tell you' mastahs
>   Dat I'se preaching' discontent.
> 'Cause I isn't; I'se a-judgin'
>   Bible people by deir ac's.
> I'se a-givin' you de Scriptuah,
>   I's a-handin' you de fac's.
> Cose ole Pher'oh b'lieved in slav'ry
>   But de Lawd he let him see,
> Dat de people he put bref in,—
>   Evah mothah's son was free.

> An' dahs othahs thinks lek Pher'oh,
>   But dey calls de Scriptuah liar,

Fuh de Bible says "a servant
        Is a-worthy of his hire."

This preacher is far from the minstrel stereotype. He is a subversive. Dunbar teaches his post-Civil War readers to deconstruct the minstrels who entertain them on stage or in collections of poetry in "Negro dialect." Invoking the supreme authority, the preacher continues:

So you see de Lawd's intention,
        Evah sence de worl' began
Was dat His almighty freedom
        Should belong to evah man.
But I think it would be bettah
        Ef I'd pause agin to say,
Dat I'm talkin' 'bout ouah freedom
        In a Biblistic way.
But de Moses is a-comin'
        An' he's comin' suah an' fas'
. . . .
        don't you git to braggin'
        'Bout dese things, you wait an' see.

Multiple messages are conveyed to multiple audiences as the preacher speaks to a faithful congregation, to the informers present and ready to run off to tell tales of conspiracy, to the indiscreet who might speak too openly of the preacher's subversive message, and to "ole Pher'oh" himself who is not paying heed to the scriptural accounts of the fate of the original Pharaoh.

Dunbar's final stanza is as subversive as his preacher's message.

But when Moses wif his powah
        Comes an' sets us chillun free,
We will praise de gracious Mastah
        Dat has gin us liberty;
An' we'll shout ouah halleluyahs
        On dat mighty reck'nin' day,
When we'se reco'nised ez citiz'—
        Huh uh! Chillun, let us pray!

In one stanza, the poet makes plain the self-awareness of the preacher and the serious intent of the preacher's words by returning to the conventional humor of dialect poetry. The preacher catches himself before he can complete the subversive word, "citizens," and calls his congregation to prayer. While "Huh uh!" is humorously spoken, "Chillun, let us pray!" is serious in its deceit. For after such a sermon, what could be prayed for but another Moses? Further, Dunbar was writing in the context of late-nineteenth-century American life, with its imposition of Jim Crow legislation and its rollback of citizenship rights for the former slaves and their descendants. His re-creation of the antebellum preacher and his sermon speaks indirectly to his own readers: My language, this plantation dialect of the minstrel show, is not only for your entertainment. It masks a more serious intent.

James Weldon Johnson, on the other hand, in his recreation of an Exodus sermon, did not trust his readers to be able to read beyond the conventions of the tortured spellings of dialect. In Johnson's view, the baggage of the minstrel tradition, with its ridicule of African American language style and its stereotyping of that language's speakers, was too much for poetry to bear. Yet Johnson argued that the folk or oral literature was one of the richest sources for a racially authentic poetry. Although Johnson had dismissed the use of "plantation dialect" as poetic language (1922, 40–41; 1927, 7), he found beauty and a wide range of expressiveness in the oral idiom. In *God's Trombones* Johnson paid homage to the poetic genius of the African American folk preacher by turning a traditional sermon cycle, such as is still being preached today, into poetry. He uses "American Standard" spellings, but his rhythms and syntax cry out for African American performance: pronunciation, intonation, and emphasis.

Johnson discussed his own technique in the "Preface" to *God's Trombones.*

> The tempos of the preacher I have endeavored to indicate by the line arrangement of the poems, and a certain sort of pause that is marked by a quick intaking and an audible expulsion of breath I have indicated by dashes. There is a decided syncopation of speech—the crowding in of many syllables or lengthening out of a few to fill one metrical foot, the sensing of which must be left to the reader's ear. The rhythmical stress of this syncopation

> ⁝ is partly obtained by a marked silent fraction of a beat; fre-
> ⁝ quently this silent fraction is filled in by a hand clap (10–11).

Johnson's elaborate stage directions are necessary, in part, because he decides not to spell out the soundings of the language. The strong rhythms of the vernacular, particularly those of the elevated language practices of the traditional church, resist easy transference to print. Johnson's performance notes, therefore, will be more meaningful to a reader who is familiar with the singsong or intoned style of preaching and testimony. This living legacy of African American sacred vernacular culture can be heard by anyone who has a radio or a compact disc or cassette player. The tradition is alive in African American church services, which are often broadcast on the radio, and on recordings of famous African American preachers, such as the Reverends C. L. Franklin and Martin Luther King Jr. Poets continue to replicate in print the sound, language, and style of the traditional sermon.

When Johnson turns to the Exodus text, he is praising by imitation Dunbar's antebellum preacher and those like him who found, and continue to find inspiration in that text. It is the artistry of the preacher, for the most part, rather than his message that is Johnson's primary focus. Nonetheless, in assuming the voice and style of a preacher, Johnson at various points in his performance also articulates the preacher's message.

> And God called Moses from the burning bush,
> He called in a still, small voice,
> And he said: Moses—Moses—
> And Moses listened,
> And he answered and said:
> Lord, here am I.

Like Dunbar, Johnson begins with the written text. By entitling his poem/sermon "Let My People Go," Johnson makes clear a second source. His title is the refrain of the great Exodus spiritual, his poem a response to its call. [5] Conflating written and oral sources, the poet claims an authorial voice that is heir to a dual tradition.

> Then God again spoke to Moses,
> And he spoke in a voice of thunder:

I am the Lord God Almighty
I am the God of thy fathers,
I am the God of Abraham,
Of Isaac and of Jacob.
And Moses hid his face.

And God said to Moses:
I've seen the awful suffering
Of my people down in Egypt.
I've watched their hard oppressors,
Their overseers and drivers;
The groans of my people have filled my ears
And I can't stand it no longer;
So I'm come down to deliver them
Out of the land of Egypt.
And I will bring them out of that land
Into the land of Canaan;
Therefore, Moses, go down,
Go down into Egypt,
And Tell Old Pharaoh
To let my people go.

Johnson here has selected typical language habits of African American English speakers, among them repetition and hypernegation (the use of double, triple, or more negatives). The preacher's language and that of the congregants, steeped in this form of expression, is "saturated with the sublime phraseology of the Hebrew prophets and steeped in the idioms of King James English . . . a fusion of Negro idioms with Bible English" (1927, 9). In the African American language community, as Smitherman points out, "whoever speaks is aware that his personality is on exhibit and his status at stake. He must have some knowledge to contribute . . . and his contribution must be presented in a dazzling, entertaining manner" (3). The preacher, as a man of words, both teaches and entertains.

Johnson's repetitions of the biblical "I am"s, the pattern of subject-verb—"I've seen . . . I've watched . . . I can't stand it"—build to "Therefore, Moses, go down, /Go down," culminating in the direct quotation of the spiritual, "Tell Old Pharaoh/To let my people go." Johnson's preacherly voice makes an old lesson new by the manner of his telling. In Smitherman's terms, he "dazzles" his listeners/readers through his manipulation of language. Through the use of repetition, a common device in oral poetry, the poet achieves the effect of the preacher to whom his poem is giving voice as he or she advances the narrative. The intensification of a statement through the double negative and the humanizing of the deity occur in the statement "I can't stand it no longer." Johnson again quotes the spiritual:

> And Moses with his rod in hand
> Went down and said to Pharaoh:
> Thus saith the Lord God of Israel,
> Let my people go.

Like its literary and oral sources, the poem testifies to the power of the word.

Johnson's efforts to convey the "personality of the preacher–his physical magnetism, his gestures and gesticulations, his changes of tempos, his pauses for effect, and more than all, his tones of voice" (*God's Trombones,* 10) are particularly effective in the following stanzas:

> Poor Old Pharaoh
> He knows all the knowledge of Egypt.
> Yet never knew—
> He never knew
> The one and the living God.
> Poor Old Pharaoh
> He's got all the power of Egypt,
> And he's going to try
> To test his strength
> With the might of the great Jehovah,
> With the might of the Lord God of Hosts,
> The Lord mighty in battle.

By means of punctuation, line length, repetition, alliteration, and vowel choice, combined with the enumeration of some of the attributes of the deity, Johnson gives voice to his preacher while at the same time providing clues for oral performance of the poem.

Johnson's preacher takes twenty-one stanzas of varying length, in contrast to Dunbar's eleven eight-line stanzas, to retell the old familiar story. The dramatic and narrative elements of the poem are clear in stanza fifteen:

In the morning,
Oh, in the morning,
They missed the Hebrew Children.
Four hundred years
Four hundred years
They'd held them down in Egypt land.
Held them without money and without price.
And it might have been Pharaoh's wife that said:
Pharaoh—look what you've done.
You let those Hebrew Children go.
And who's going to serve us now?
Who's going to make our bricks and mortar?
Who's going to plant and plow our corn?
Who's going to get up in the chill of the morning?
And who's going to work in the blazing sun?
Pharaoh, tell me that!

(If ever Johnson's decision to use standard spellings fails him, it is in these last five lines. Their rhythm demands a pronunciation of "gonna" or "gon" for "going to.") As in previous dialogues between Moses and Pharaoh (stanzas 7 and 13) and between Moses and the Lord (stanzas 1 through 5 and stanza 12), one can hear distinctly different voices. (The "Hebrew Children" speak in stanzas 9 and 18.) In each of these instances, it is clear that the preacher is giving dramatic voice to his characters. The use of dialogue to advance elements of plot is a tried and true element of oral narrative or story telling. The use of story as an element of sermon is equally common. Johnson's use of elements of orality or orature in the service of the written word extends the oral tradition into writing.

In the final stanza of the poem, the preacherly voice of the sermon/poem seems to merge with that of the preacher/poet.

Listen!—Listen!
All you sons of Pharaoh.
    Who do you think can hold God's people
When the Lord God himself has said
Let my people go?

A single authoritative voice addresses an audience external to the assumed congregation of the poem's world, an audience, moreover, which needs to be reminded of the enduring relevance of the classic story. The worlds of religious faith—the biblical story—and historical memory—the metaphorical identification of enslaved Africans with enslaved Jews—offer a contemporary lesson. At the same time, the poet teaches a lesson in language practice.

The traditional religious revival evoked through the poems of *God's Trombones* are New World equivalents of what Gerald Haslam describes as an African language event, in which literary creation is central. Like the performance of a traditional African griot or storyteller, the prayers, testimony, and sermons of the revival are elements of a "joyous, intense interchange in which language [is] employed to elicit the sacred and to offer release and solace to the congregation" (Haslam, 4). As the participants in the event communicate meaning through words, the event itself celebrates the word.

Just as the retellings of the Exodus story are in many ways self-reflexive meditations on the power of language itself, so the subject and themes associated with affirmations of the legacy of *nommo*—the empowering, engendering word—are part of the African American poetic tradition. In 1961 the English translation of Janheinz Jahn's *Muntu: An Outline of the New African Culture* was published in the United States. This work, which posits the cultural unity of Africa and its diaspora, proposes as a common element a belief in *nommo,* the word. Included in that concept are notions of the word as power and the word as tool. When the Lord says, "Let my people go," the word engenders the deed. Poets of the New Black Arts movement,[6] particularly members of the writers' workshop of the Organization of Black American Culture (OBAC) in Chicago, saw themselves as transmitters of *nommo.*

Two poems by Gwendolyn Brooks, both written during the peak of the Black Arts movement, are illustrative. "The Sermon on the Warpland" (printed in her *Blacks*) exhorts its readers to "Say that the River turns, and turn the River." The eulogy "Martin Luther King, Jr." (printed in Adoff) praises the famed preacher for his word power:

The word was Justice. It was spoken.
So it shall be spoken.
So it shall be done.

The spoken word not only precedes action, it also causes action. Brooks's "River," often taken to stand for the cultural (perhaps literary?) mainstream, can be turned from its course by the communal utterance. Similarly, in the eulogy for Martin Luther King Jr., the word "Justice" has been spoken and shall be spoken until it comes to be. Words have power that endures after they are spoken or written, even after the death of the speaker or the publication of the poem. (Brooks's poems in the sermonic mode, her preachments, are discussed at greater length in chapter 3 of this study.) What is significant is the identification of the preacher/poet as one who articulates a communal voice and as one whose words have the power to engender a new reality.

Thus far I have described some of the ways in which African American poets extend vernacular practices into their poetry. The poets make use of the full continuum of language as spoken by African Americans. The choice of where along the continuum of language a poet chooses to situate a poem is dictated by the situation, that is, the occasion that gives rise to the poem, as well as the audience that is assumed to be hearing or reading the poem. Further, the voice in which the poet chooses to articulate the poem also governs where along the language continuum a poem rests. For example, the flourishes and ornamentation of the sermonic mode found in "An Ante-Bellum Sermon" and "Let My People Go" would not be appropriate for another kind of language event, such as the telling of a tall tale or the singing of a blues lyric. African American poets extend the griot, or bardic, tradition by performing their poetry in formal and informal readings and recitations before audiences. The silent reader, too, becomes an active participant in the language situation as she or he hears with the inner ear and praises (or dismisses) the written text.

Negotiating the space between the written page and the oral performance, the African American poet engages the written language in oral terms. Through the use of superallusive mascons and figures and performance modes drawn from vernacular culture, the poet achieves a kind of written orality. Writing in the presence of an implicit community/congregation, the poet writes responses to both oral and written cultural calls; the call-and-response structures are written into the poems themselves. In its language practice and in its performative nature, African American poetry and its making extend vernacular cultural practice. The poetry performs the word.

CHAPTER 2

Orality

Language and Voice

Academic discussions of African American literary tradition and other African world literary traditions tend to privilege oral tradition as the ancestor of the written literature. At the same time, current academic practice ranks text and narrative as "better" than mere oral tradition. My discussion of African American poetry as vernacular culture would seem to assign primacy to orality. However, my argument is more complicated. Orality is not more authentic because it comes first. In fact, we cannot say that orality is more authentic than literacy. But neither can we say that writing—and its technology, print—is of greater intellectual value because it is an organized system of recording language. Writing and print do enable a language to have rules assigned to it, to develop a written tradition and a somewhat more lasting record. Yet modern electronic methods of recording the spoken word also lend permanence to language and literature. The complicated relationship between orality and the written/recorded word must be teased out to clarify the nature of orality itself.

Walter B. Ong, in his discussion of *Orality and Literacy* (1982), asserts that "written texts all have to be related somehow, directly or indirectly, to the world of sound, the natural habitat of language, to yield their meanings" (8). Yet "to this day no concepts have yet been formed for effectively, let alone gracefully, conceiving of oral art as such without reference, conscious or unconscious, to writing" (10). African American poets write out of a vernacular tradition that particularly values the sounds of language. The style of *sounding* the language, as much as the language itself, communicates meaning.

Contemporary discussions of orature tend to focus on the verbal expressive arts of preliterate or nonliterate cultures. Literature assumes literacy and print. African American orature, however, exists in a realm of duality, a kind of double consciousness.[1] Much of African American literature is written to be read aloud (preferably to an audibly responsive audience). The African American writer centers a speaking voice in a written text very often through the presentation of a dramatic scenario. Similarly, African American vernacular culture manifests itself simultaneously in the realms of orality and literacy. Collections of lyrics of spirituals, blues, and proverbial sayings were published as early as the nineteenth century. Today, texts of popular song lyrics and rap lyrics accompany the recordings. And recitations and readings of works of literature are commonplace on African American school and church programs. The would-be hip consult lexicons of African American language and collections of folk sayings and street repartee (e.g., Major; Smitherman, 1994). The intertextuality of print and oral/electronic media cultures is an observable phenomenon. Whether "Black English" is perceived as a dialect or as a language is less important than the fact that African American vernacular exists as a cultural marker and vehicle for expressivity.

I use the term *African American vernacular culture* to refer to those customs and mores that appear to be most specifically manifested by persons in the United States who trace their ancestry to Africans enslaved there. Orality is only one aspect of that culture, a vehicle of cultural expressivity and performance. Mineke Schipper identifies a "written orality . . . the transposition of characteristic features of oral discourse into the written text. . . . In order to appreciate [those features] adequately, one needs to study them with 'ear philology' as well as with 'eye philology'" (66). When we read African American poetic texts informed by such an ear philology, we can hear that, while they are taken from vernacular speech, they do not mimic that speech; rather, they create a written analog for it. Aldon Nielsen describes these texts as "musicked speech, written down, relined and re-presented as visual texts" (127). His description points to the ways in which the poets make their texts sing and turn everyday talk into poetry, using words as both soundings and signs.

So, what is the relationship between a vernacular, mostly oral, tradition and a literary, mostly written one? Nielsen offers an alternative way to identify these traditions, namely "voicing and scripting" (22). The African American poet uses scriptings as a way to communicate voicings. Writing is an extension of speaking or singing. African world cultures value word skills, poetry making, story telling, and the literary extensions of these more public activities; they rely on an audience that is hearing as well as reading. The history of wordplay in African American vernacular culture illustrates these tendencies. The current dominance of rap culture among African American youth, who originated the form, manifests the importance of wordplay in the culture, as do the continuing traditions of prayer, testimony, and sermon in the traditional church and the high value ascribed to oratorical skill as a qualification for African American leadership. The ability of a leader to "talk the talk" is often a credential for elected office or for moral or social authority

Orality is a communal expression: African American audiences talk back to movie screens, television screens, and radios as if the speakers were physically present. The "Amen Corner"[2] translates into the secular sphere at every concert venue and at theater performances as well. Call elicits response in African American vernacular culture. A written text can function as a call. Texts can call and respond to each other as well as to their readers. Individual writers provide variations on common vernacular and literary themes. In the manner of individual soloists in a jazz group, African American writers enter an ongoing conversation.

For example, Gwendolyn Brooks places Don L. Lee in the Mecca in her long poem of that name, while he sings her praises in several of his poems. The blues poems dialogue with each other and classic and traditional blues lyrics. And poet after poet reflects on the dynamics of the train, John Coltrane, in the lives of African Americans. Thus, the African American writer codifies and regularizes African American orality by bringing it into the realm of the printed word. In African American culture, a literary work often exists to be performed. African American ways of speaking, intoning, and singing words lurk within the forms of African American poetry.

African American poetry displays many characteristics more usually attributed to oral poetry. Ruth Finnegan, in her definitive 1977 work, describes oral poetry as "that which circulates by oral rather than written means; in contrast to written poetry, its distribution, composition, or performance are by word of mouth and not through reliance on the written or printed word" (16). Further, she writes, "a piece of oral literature, to reach its full actualization, must be performed" (28). My earliest experience of the poetry of Paul Laurence Dunbar and Langston Hughes was in performance. I heard their words performed before I ever saw them in print. It was such performances and public readings that drew me to the written texts and introduced me to other works by the poets. (Earlier, I have noted the poetry recitation as one of the popular performance sites of African American vernacular culture.) Finnegan distinguishes oral from written poetry, claiming that oral poetry is "more flexible and more dependent on social context," more dependent on the "nature of the audience, context of performance, personality of poet-performer, and the details of the performance itself" (29). Such distinctions blur if we examine public readings by African American poets of their own work.[3] Poets become performers of their work, interacting with their audiences in a type of communal ritual of call and response. The public or televised poetry reading, the spoken word/poetry video (as seen, for example, on MTV), often provides impetus for the purchase of a book of poems, showing how the spoken and written words partake of each other.

Finnegan's observations about the relationship between oral poetic prosody and that of written poetry are particularly germane. According to Finnegan, oral poetry shares with written poetry certain elements of prosody such as "alliteration, assonance, rhyme, tonal repetitions or even parallelism" (90) as well as meter or rhythm. Oral poetry makes significant uses of repetition, including call and response, chorus or refrain, and incremental repetition. Favored stanzaic patterns are couplet, triplet, and quatrain. Particularities of language or diction include "imagery and symbolic language, figurative language, simile, metaphor, personification, hyperbole, allusion, and modes of expression such as the first person voicing, dialogue, and third person narration" (112–117). Finally, Finnegan describes the interaction between oral and written poetry as "extremely common. . . . The idea that the use of writing *automatically* deals a death blow to oral literary forms has nothing to support it" (160).

It is characteristic of many African American poets self-consciously to make use of the forms of oral tradition: epic, ballad or short narrative, panegyric ode or praise song, and short lyric. They also employ many of the stylistic elements of oral poetry Finnegan cites. The repetition of these forms and usages across differences of generation and gender argue for the existence of a definable literary convention and tradition.

If we explore further the relation of language and literary practice with culture, the relationship between characteristic language practices of African American culture and poetic language begins to emerge.

Adrian A. Roscoe, in *Mother Is Gold* (1971), lists various attributes of West African language and culture that easily might be applied to African American language practice. Language, he writes, is a "key to man's inner being . . . a mirror of social standing . . . an instrument of deceit and oppression . . . a device for sheer entertainment . . . a vehicle for man's deepest utterances . . . a source of comedy . . . an instrument of satire" (244). Again, although these observations might encompass the full range of human language practice, African American vernacular speech and other Black vernaculars seem more self-reflexive and self-conscious. Their language practice serves as a site of resistance to cultural dominance, even as they speak the "masters'" language. Through language practice, the individual claims membership in a group and affirms a way of speaking and being in the world.

Geneva Smitherman (1975), in her discussion of the sacred and secular registers of African American vernacular, defines the origins of the sacred style as "rural and Southern," describing it as "more emotional and highly charged than the secular style, which she describes as "urban and Northern" although with Southern and rural roots (15). What the sacred and secular traditions share, according to Smitherman, are rhetorical commonalities of call and response, songified patterns, and signification. "Black English" or African American vernacular speech, she asserts, is "a linguistic code, an entire rappin [sic] style shot through with ambiguity, irony, paradox, and bound to the immediate linguistic context as well as to the context of Black enslavement in White America" (7). Stylistic elements of the code include a semantics grounded in the "socio-psychological space between the words" (8). Further, this language has it own "lexicon" consisting of English words, including profanity, "which have potentially two levels of meaning . . . [and] within the Black level, many sub-levels" (10). Smitherman traces the multiple levels of meaning to the necessity during slavery for the use of coded language. Paul Laurence Dunbar "Ante-Bellum Sermon" (discussed in chapter 1) is illustrative of this practice. What has evolved is "metaphorical and imagistic ways of communicating" with "figurative power and rhetorical beauty . . . to complement its survival functionality" (Smitherman 13).

Stephen Henderson posits a "lingustic elegance" to this language with characteristic usages including "jazzy rhythmic effects, virtuoso free rhyming with an emphasis on wordplay, hyperbolic imagery, metaphysical imagery, understatement, compressed and cryptic imagery. And worrying the line" (33–41). Worrying the line, the repetition of sounds, words, and phrases, is particularly significant. The term is taken from the world of African American music, in which the singer or soloist repeats a word or phrase while varying the rhythm or melody. Dillard notes "elements of conscious elegantizing: the use of intentionally glittering and susquepedelian words and phrases and the types of disregard for dictionary precision of meaning" observable among African American folk preachers and political orators (146–147). This African American language practice is analogous to the Black Caribbean "Fancy Talk" observed by Abraham and Szwed. They note a tendency in Black speakers to "flavor their everyday discourse with set speeches, effusive patterns of movement and proverbs" (78). Choosing words for the way they sound or the way they fill the mouth is a practice of many African American poets.

Elsewhere, Dillard identifies other characteristic language practices rooted in West African language and culture, such as West Africian naming practices. "Day names, birth order names, job names, gift names describing wished for or developed characteristics" (134) may be the African vernacular source for African American names such as "Simple."[4] The man who was born LeRoy Jones renamed himself first LeRoi (did he think of himself as a king?), then Imamu (spiritual leader) Ameer (prince) Baraka (blessed), and then (finally?) Amiri Baraka—dropping the spiritual leader to become, in "gift names describing wished for or developed characteristics," a more African-named blessed prince. Abraham and Szwed too note "strange naming practices" and a "widespread employment of proverbs" in eighteenth- and nineteenth-century accounts of how slaves talked among themselves (81–91). Such observable parallels among language practices of the Black English-speaking world are commonplace; the subject is ripe for further study.

Smitherman, like Dillard, observes the vernacular practice of double negatives as intensifiers. "There are two patterns of negation in Black language that differentiate it from White speech . . . triple and quadruple negatives, for example 'nobody don't never' and 'ain't nobody never,' and 'limited negation' as in 'don't nobody but' or 'don't but'" (1975, 32). "Ain't but me one" is the refrain of an old slave song.

All linguistic studies of African American vernacular note the "speech rhythms, voice inflections and tonal patterns" (Smitherman, 1975, 39) of the language. (Cf. Johnson's discussion in *God's Trombones.*) Many trace the origins of these characteristic usages to African tonal languages. Claude Brown, in "The Language of Soul" (in Kochman, 1972) argues for the importance of pronunciation, stress and intonation as defining characteristics of African American vernacular. For example, the meaning of the English word "bad" is transformed into its opposite in African American vernacular through stress, pitch, and elongation of the vowel.

Finally, Dillard isolates hyperbole as characteristic of African American vernacular. Continuing his discussion of the oratorical style of "fancy talk," he describes a poetic diction or highly seasoned talk with a "flashy vocabulary, often beyond appropriateness to the subject under discussion from the point of view of the speaker of Standard English" (249). Such "oratorical splendor," Dillard claims, is "an Africanism" (251). Smitherman, too, identifies the vernacular appreciation for the "flamboyant, flashy and exaggerative" in language practice, describing vernacular speakers as "highly stylized dramatic and spectacular" (1975, 3). Henderson's description of the "living speech of the Black Community" also notes the cultural proclivity for hyperbole.

African American poets, by selecting vernacular expression as the favored poetic language, infuse their art with a cultural specificity. The poet's selection of the mother tongue, moreover, asserts a sociopolitical identification with the group that shares the language. The implications of the existence of a language continuum are many. Popular notions of what constitutes "Negro dialect" or "Ebonics"[5] place limitations on actual African American linguistic practice. The idea of a language continuum gives us a way to describe the wide range of linguistic options from which African American poets might choose. Educated African Americans often speak a variety of Englishes dependent upon the time, place, audience, or situation. Dillard makes a distinction between "ethnic slang" and "Black English": the former, he says, is used by African Americans whose English is most standard "as a means of retaining some feature of ethnic solidarity" (242). Henderson, Rohlehr, and I, on the other hand, would say that the use of ethnic slang is merely one stop along a continuum of vernacular language practice. It is, then, in the varied uses of language in a community that I situate African American vernacular speech, the mother tongue. Like its mother tongue, African American poetry is a vehicle for cultural expressivity.

Paul Laurence Dunbar achieved fame in the late nineteenth century in the United States for what he would later characterize as "jingles in a broken tongue" (275). Marcellus Blount has argued persuasively that Dunbar subversively reclaims African American plantation vernacular from the oppressive conventions of blackface minstrelsy. The Local Color movement, of which Dunbar was a member, gave rise to an increasing amount of regional and dialect poetry in the United States. Dunbar actually was in the American literary mainstream when he began to write in dialect. Although his dialect poetry partakes of some of the elements of the popular stage of his day, Dunbar uses dialect to fill in the warmth, humor, and humanity of the slaves. In doing so, he replicates in writing a culturally specific way of using language—double-voicedness or indirection, a kind of verbal duplicity. While one audience might read a simple stereotyping, another might read a more complex human being.

Grace Sims Holt discusses this type of language practice as a kind of "linguistic subversion" ("'Inversion,'" in Kochman, 1972). The purpose of the game, she argues, was "to appear to but not to" (154). She points out that African Americans use "double-meaning as a verbal device to deceive whites" (159). Dunbar's dialect speakers, rather than being objects of ridicule, are the subjects of his explorations of the warmth, humor, and sentiment of ordinary people at home and at play. Their words are the written equivalent of the mother tongue in which Dunbar had probably heard tales of life on the plantation from his parents, former slaves. His nostalgia is that with which each generation looks back on the "olden days." However, when Dunbar wants to evoke the sublime— the dignity, the pain, the suffering, the visionary—he turns to the literary language of his time. An examination of Dunbar's three poems in tribute to the "colored troops" of the Civil War illustrates his double-voicedness. "When Dey 'Listed Colored Soldiers" is a dramatic monologue spoken in dialect by a woman whose lover, named Lias, has enlisted in the Union Army.

> Dey was talkin' in de cabin, dey was
>   talkin' in de hall;
> But I listened kin' o' keerless, not
>   a-t'inkin' 'bout it all;
> An' on Sunday, too, I noticed, dey was
>   whisp'rin' mighty much,
> Stan'in' all erroun' de roadside w'en dey
>   let us out o' chu'ch.

> But I didn't t'ink erbout it 'twell de mid-
>   dle of de week,
> An' my 'Lias come to see me, an' somehow
>   he couldn't speak.
> Den I seed all in a minute whut he'd come
>   to see me for:—
> Dey had 'listed colo'ed sojers, an my 'Lias
>   gwine to wah.

The poem, with its inconsistent spelling system, might be described as sentimental, even "pathetic" in its rendering of the pride of the young recruit and the mixed feelings of the woman who shares his pride, but remains on the plantation to worry and wait. Behind the poem, Dunbar gives voice to a speaker who is unseen, unheard, and unknown.

Dunbar's Standard English poems, "The Colored Soldiers" and "The Unsung Heroes," on the other hand, have a different purpose and are rendered from a different point along the language continuum. "The Colored Soldiers" begins, "If the muse were mine to tempt it," and goes on to praise the "noble sons of Ham" who "were comrades then and brothers/ Are they more or less to-day?" "The Unsung Heroes," too, is a public hymn of praise.

> A song for the unsung heroes who rose in
>   the country's need,
> When the life of the land was threatened
>   by the slaver's cruel greed,
> For the men who came from the cornfield,
>   who came from the plough and the flail,
> Who rallied round when they heard the sound
>   of the mighty man of the rail.
> They laid them down in the valleys, they
>   laid them down in the wood,
> And the world looked on at the work they
>   did, and whispered, "It is good."
> They fought their way on the hillside, they
>   fought their way in the glen,
> And God looked down on their sinews brown,
>   and said, "I have made them men."

. . . .
Give, thou, some seer the power to sing
    them in their might,
The men who feared the master's whip,
    but did not fear the fight;
That he may tell of thier virtues
    as min-strels did of old,
Till the pride of face and the hate of race
    grow obsolete and cold.

Both "The Unsung Heroes" and "The Colored Soldiers" are as much poems about making poetry as they are about the subjects being praised. They sing in the language of the schoolroom and the public platform in order to render the appropriate homage. On the other hand, "When Dey 'Listed Colored Soldiers" gives voice to a speaking subject proclaiming in her own voice a common emotional experience. White Civil War wives, widows, sweethearts, mothers, and sisters could identify with its sentiment, complex in its mixture of pride and grief. It is the subject's language, as much as its particulars of time and occasion, that tells us who is speaking, when, and why. In the latter two poems, on the other hand, it is the poet himself in his public voice who speaks/sings a public song of praise. Like the dialect poem, the praise songs contain not too subtle arguments for racial equality.

When James Weldon Johnson repudiated "Negro dialect," he did so with full recognition of the richness of "folk expression" or vernacular speech as a source of poetic idiom. In *God's Trombones,* he attempted to replicate the idioms, cadences, metaphors, and rhythms of the mother tongue as prayed, testified, and preached. It is in the "folk" language events of prayer, testimony, and sermon, that Johnson situated his poems. Such language events, claims Roger Abrahams in his discussion of "the man of words," furnish the sites of a performance aesthetic held and shared by a speaker and his audience (in Kochman, 1972). So successful is Johnson in re-creating the language of the church that performers of his text often use vernacular pronunciation rather than the Standard English pronunciations that his spellings would seem to demand.[6]

And as far as the eye of God could see
Darkness covered everything.

> Blacker than a hundred midnights
> Down in a cypress swamp.

So effective has Johnson been in evoking the preacherly style and the African American language situations of prayer and sermon, that he evokes the down-home pronunciation too. The pattern of stressed and unstressed syllables mimics the rhythms of the singsong style commonplace in the traditional church service.

Johnson's distaste for dialect as literary language seems to be rooted in the way it appears on the page—misspelled, mispronounced English. He is overly sensitive to racial outsiders' condemnations of "bad English" as evidence of racial inferiority. Johnson also articulates the historically ambivalent attitude of "the folk" themselves about the relative value of "good" and "bad" English. Current arguments in the African American community about treating Standard English as a "second language" in its instruction reflects the ongoing nature of this discussion.

Abrahams's discussion (in Kochman) of similar language practices in the Caribbean identifies two types: "one emphasizes joking and license, and the other centers on decorum and formality. The former emphasizes bringing the vernacular Creole into stylized use, in the form of wit, repartee, and directed slander. The latter is a demonstration of the speaker's abilities in standard English, but strictly on the elaborate oratorical level" (219).

Double consciousness, an awareness of the audience from outside the culture that may be judging language practices by a different standard, leads to a condemnation or critique rooted in elitism or class bias. The mother tongue is the language of the often-unlettered masses, and they often view use of the standard as "talking white." What dialect or vernacular speech affords the poet, then, is the verbal authenticity of his own "folk." When such poetry is read aloud on the radio, on television, or on stage, the "folk" recognize their mother tongue and are predisposed to listen, hear, and heed.[7] The poet speaks/writes to give voice to the group.

Thomas Kochman's essay (in his edited volume) on African American vernacular "verbal behavior" identifies eight language practices.[8] Of those practices, "signifying" is central to any discussion of African American poetic practice. *Signifying* in Kochman's terms is "provocation, goading and taunting"; although its function is "directive, the tactic which is employed is one of indirection" (257). Geneva Smitherman agrees with Kochman, describing "signifyin" as "ritualized insult, a verbal put-down. . . . [It is] a way of talking about somebody through indirection . . . [and] also a way of teaching without preaching . . . characterized by exploitation of the unexpected and quick verbal surprise. . . . Employing under-statement and metaphor, the signifier always conveys his message through humor (1975, 22). Smitherman further defines *signifyin* as "putting down [one's] enemies in the audience without direct frontal attack" (7). Her use of the male pronoun in this case is not inclusive but gender specific. The combative aspects of signifying as vernacular practice often relegate it to the male sphere. She then goes on to identify other vernacular language practices such as "rhythmic or songified pattern [s] . . . demonstrating verbal dexterity" (8) and the rap, which was"originally romantic talk . . . for the purposes of winning [a woman's] emotional and sexual affection; testifyin [or] symbolic ritual in which the speaker may unravel his deeds and life story or give witness to the efficacy, truth and power of some experiences in which his audience has also shared; [and] reversal [in which] whatever the word means in White America, it takes the opposite meaning in Black America" (11–12).

Claudia Mitchell-Kernan (in Kochman) expands Kochman's and Smitherman's analyses of signifying to apply to the context of the verbal behavior of women and mixed groups as well as that of young males: "Signifying, however, also refers to a way of encoding messages or meanings, which involves, in most cases, an element of indirection . . . an alternative message form, selected for its artistic merit [which] may occur embedded in a variety of discourses" (315).

For Mitchell-Kernan, the defining characteristic of this vernacular language practice is its "metaphorical reference" (326). The apparent meaning *signifies* the actual meaning. Hence the importance of "shared cultural knowledge for [the] correct semantic interpretation" (327).

"Playing the dozens" is an even more gender-specific language practice of African American vernacular culture. Smitherman defines this practice as a "ritualized kind of verbal game that involves talking disparagingly about someone's mother . . . [and] by analogy to include other relatives and even ancestors. . . . [T]he objective is to better your opponent with more caustic humorous 'insults' . . . [through] a competitive test of linguistic ingenuity and verbal fluency in which the winner, determined by the audience's responses, becomes a culture hero" (24). The public and communal aspects of playing the dozens provide culturally specific context and rhetorical history for the current phenomena of the poetry slam and jazz or hiphop "cutting contests."[9]

Geneva Smitherman also describes the "toast," which I discuss at greater length in chapter 5, as "a narrative folk tale, complete with rhymed lines and poetic imagery—gutsy and sexual . . . a tribute to the hero, who is usually a fearless defiant Black man—what Black folk approvingly call a 'bad niggah.' . . . Told in epic fashion, the movement of the Toast proceeds episodically with the overriding theme being the omnipotence of Black folk as symbolized in the lone figure of the Black hero" (1975, 25). The toast gives structure to numerous popular songs and published poems, such as those by H. Rap Brown, Langston Hughes, and Ishmael Reed. "Because of their earthy language and content, both the Dozens and the Toast have traditionally been relegated to 'low-life street talk'" (Smitherman, 1975, 26)." H. Rap Brown, in his 1969 autobiography, *Die Nigger Die,* discusses the various forms of "street talk" (see his essay in Kochman, 1972). "Rap's Poem," arranged in poem form by Stephen Henderson (187–188), is like the raps of many young, urban African American men during the fifties and early sixties and demonstrates the form's urban folk roots:

> I'm the man who walked the water and tied the whale's tale
> in a knot
> Taught the little fishes how to swim
> Crossed the burning sands and shook the devil's hand
> Rode around the world on the back of a snail carrying a sack
> saying AIR MAIL.

The boasting contents of such raps are the antecedents of contemporary recorded rap and provide a model form for such poems as Nikki Giovanni's "Ego tripping" (*Re: Creation,* 1970) and Ishmael Reed's "I Am a Cowboy in the Boat of Ra" (*Catechism,* 1970):

> I was born in the congo
> I walked to the fertile crescent and built the sphinx
> I designed a pyramid so tough that a star
> that only glows every one hundred years falls
> into the center giving divine perfect light
> I am bad

> I am a cowboy in the boat of Ra. Boning-up in
> the ol West I bide my time. . . .
>
> . . . .
>
> . . . Women arrive
> on the backs of goats and throw themselves on
> my Bowie.

These poems illustrate the pervasiveness of the performative or dramatic impulses in vernacular expressive culture, including the use of profanity, which figured in street personae of the New Black Arts poets. Henderson cites profanity in African American vernacular and poetry as an "appropriation of the dozens technique" (42). The dozens has been compared in studies by anthropologists and folklorists to poetry and rituals of insult in West Africa. African American poets have raised insult and invective to high art.[10] The legacy of their poetic practice lives on in contemporary hiphop culture.

> Jo jo was modern/ an international nigger
>   born: jan. 1, 1863 in new york, mississippi.
> His momma was mo militant than he was/is
> jo jo bes no instant negro
> his development took all of 106 years
>   Haki Madhubuti, poem from
>   *We Walk the Way of the New World*

> this is for u insect w / no antennae, goofy
> papers piling on yr desk—for u & others. Where
> do u fugitives frm d file cabinet of death get
> off in yr attempt to control d artist?
> keep yr programming to those computers u love so
> much, for he who meddles w/nigro-mancers
> courts his demise!
>   Ishmael Reed, *Catechism of a*
>   *NeoAmerican Hoodoo Church*

Smitherman (1975) notes the class associations in the use of this type of language in her discussions of signifyin, the dozens, and the toast. This identification of racial authenticity with outlaw, street, or lumpen[11] mores has its contemporary counterpart in African American and white suburban youths' adoption of the trappings of hiphop and gangsta rap culture. In fact, African American youths' gangsta style has become a worldwide phenomenon.

In addition to its language practices, African American vernacular culture has its own performance style. Molefe Asante, in *The Afrocentric Idea* (1987), isolates elements of "rhythm, styling and sound" as components of African American rhetorical style, including "regular clustering of tones according to accent and time value" (38). Asante identifies indirection and polyrhythm, intonation and tonal stylings, and improvisation as elements of African American oral style. In hypothesizing a "metatheory" of Black Rhetoric, he identifies "three components to code structuring in the rhetorical behavior of Black Americans" as "lyrical quality, vocal artifact, and indirection" (43). This behavior, this way of using language, shares many of the characteristics of poetry. Asante goes on to relate "Afrocentric presentation forms" to music, "particularly the epic styles of blues and jazz" with improvisation as the "soul of performance" (54). Clarence Major, in the introduction to his dictionary of African American slang (1994), asserts that "how words *sound* has always interested black speakers" (xxix). A "written orality" is achieved for African American poetry in the intersection of oral and aural, sound and appearance.

It is not only its sounds and ways of using language that African American poetry derives from the vernacular. Gayl Jones (1991) writes that "imaginative literature . . . deliberately derives its themes, language, design and vision from oral literature" (2). In African American literature, Jones finds a "more manifest and deliberate use of oral tradition and folklore to achieve and assert a distinctive aesthetic and literary voice" (7). The theme, design, and vision, infused into the vernacular flow, into the language and performance style. Jones notes the wide range of vernacular practice in her analysis of a jazz poetic suite by Michael Harper. She explains that "not all poetry using oral tradition chooses dialect; it may choose the formal orchestrations, values, and tonal contexts" (54) of that tradition. Jones's use of the language of music criticism to describe poetry is not unusual. African American poetry's relationship to music and song is a manifestation of the poet's rendering of voice. The African American poet's grounding in orality and vernacular language and performance styles lets him or her articulate the culturally specific—the poet gives voice to the people out of whom he or she emerges. The performative nature of

African American vernacular culture provides a context out of which the poet can construct his or her art.

Marcellus Blount, in his discussion of Dunbar's "Ante-Bellum Sermon," points out that many black poets "have made the vernacular sermonic performance of their heritage a primary site of cultural authority and artistic creativity" (584). Vernacular performance as a site of both authority and authenticity as well as artistic creativity is essential to an understanding of African American literature. Abrahams and Szwed, describing a similarity between African American and Caribbean language practice, cite "the use of talk to proclaim the presence of self, to assert oneself vocally in the most unguarded situations. . . . We are shown the value of arguing in the daily prosecution of life as one technique of dramatizing oneself. . . ." This use of talk reveals "a view of the importance of a high formal and decorous approach to language in . . . intercultural exhanges" (77–78); that is, language is a way of asserting oneself in the presence of another culture. Further, Rohlehr distinguishes between the folk or peasant culture and an oral culture that may be both working and middle class, as in the events of the sermon or the tea meeting speech with their "high rhetoric" or "fancy talk." "The important link between each element," Rohlehr argues, "is that of *voice* [which] signals the constant presence and pressure of people living immediate unabstracted lives" (12). The African American poet translates these voices and voicings into writing.

The preeminence of the first-person speaking voice in much of African American poetry is central to its orality and performativity or drama. More than merely poetic personae, the voices in these poems provide the literary equivalent of "speaking in tongues." Whether the "I" is an individual or communal voice, it carries its own authority. Garrett Stewart (1990) posits "the idea of an 'embodied' voice [which] emerges . . . signaling the very *destination* of the text in the reading act, the medium, of its silent voicing, sounding board rather than source" (3). This speaking/singing voice claims authorship of the text. In a narrative of personal experience or testimony, the poet uses a "hear me talking to you" mode of discourse common in the folk tale and sermon, embedding a call-and-response pattern into the written text. Like the unknown creators of the texts of spirituals and blues lyrics, the African American poet creates texts that are meant to be heard (as well as read).

I am the smoke king
I am black
    W.E.B. Du Bois, "The Song of the Smoke"
                    (1899; in Adoff)

I, too, sing America.
    Langston Hughes (c. 1925)

i
am going to rise
en masse
from Inner City
                Mari Evans,"Vive Noir! (in
                I Am a Black Woman, 1968)

I learned my body early. I can make it
crawl into the music and work from the inside out.
I was built wide and mellow,
I'm boneless to find the drumbeat.
        Patricia Smith, "Slow Dance" (in *Life*
           According to Motown, 1991)

These poems, written over a period of about a hundred years, have in common a first-person speaker. They share the characteristics of conversion narrative, testimony, or blues lyric. The poets testify in terms of identity, ancestry, or heritage as surely as the saved convert whose "testimony" begins, "I have always been a sheep. I was never a goat. I was created and cut out and born in the world for heaven. Even before God freed my soul and told me to go, I was never hell-scared. I just never did feel that my soul was made to burn in hell" (C. H. Johnson, 58). Just as testimony details how the saved convert "got ovah" Jordan from sin to grace or salvation, the African American poet testifies to the experiences that have enabled her or him to cross over to survival, triumph, or transcendence. It is in the convergence of the individual testifying voice and the communal witnessing reader/ congregation that orality is rendered literary.

The Poetry of Preachment

Didacticism in African American Poetry

*"I've got a home up inna dat kingdom
    Ain'a dat good news."*
TRADITIONAL

"How many years since 1619 . . . ?"
MARGARET WALKER

"Speak the Truth to the People."
MARI EVANS

"Say that the River turns, and turn the River."
GWENDOLYN BROOKS

Linkages between the oral tradition of vernacular culture and poetry are many and varied. While the relation of African American poetry to musical forms such as the spiritual, the blues, and jazz has received some critical attention (see Baker, 1994, 1984; G. Jones, 1991; S. A. Williams, in Fisher and Stepto, 1979), a less-explored terrain in the vernacular culture is found in the world of African American sacred expression, the traditional church. I use "traditional church" to refer to vernacular performance styles of worship common among African American evangelical Protestant congregations. I refer in particular to the heart of the church service, the language, performance, or speech act of the sermon. Bruce A. Rosenberg has argued, in the 1970 study *The Art of the American Folk Preacher,* that the sermon, especially as performed by the Southern preacher, is a type of oral poetry. Rosenberg's observations on the composition process, stylistic elements, and performance techniques of this indigenous art form situate an essentially oral art form, more commonly described as a form of folk culture, in the context of a modern literate society. Further, he shows an oral form of expression intersects with print and electronic modes of expression. Dolan Hubbard traces the influence of the sermonic mode of expression on African American narrative texts in his 1994 study *The Sermon and the African American Literary Imagination:* "The genius of the black sermon is that it transforms the discrete aspects of black expression from a system of signs, songs, and stories to an oral, expressive, unifying document that conveys a shared value system. The ritualized aspect of the sermon becomes myth . . . an existential reality—and thus gains social authority to create and disseminate cultural values" (15).

Preaching as an expressive art has a long history in African American vernacular culture. Rosenberg traces its form and spirit to both the New England Puritan sermon form and the more widespread spirit of the Second Great Awakening of American Protestantism. Hubbard assigns a more culturally specific role to the sermon: "As a direct result of their exclusion from full participation in American society, African Americans attempted to redefine themselves and their history through speech acts. Grounded in the church and based to a large extent on improvisation, these speech acts, keyed to the preacher's speech act, provided the aesthetic underpinnings for black oral expression" (4). The sermon, in African American vernacular culture, is viewed as serious artistic activity—a multifaceted, multipurposeful use of language, an exercise in verbal virtuosity, evidence of both the authority and calling of the preacher. Each preacher has a distinctive voice and style. There are, however, some constants among the sermons of great African American preachers in terms of their use of language and their performance styles. The best sermons are filled with hyperbolic language, apostrophe, fantastic imagery, incantatory repetitions, puns and rhymes. Changing rhythmic patterns indicate shifts in tone or content. Storytelling, either of biblical tales or stories drawn from everyday experience, is a primary structural element. Sometimes the story constitutes the text, or organizing theme, for the sermon. At other times, the story is used to clarify or illustrate a particular point in the sermon. Finally, the African American folk sermon is communal and visceral, expressive of the emotions of the preacher and congregation, as opposed to private and intellectual. The sermon speaks to hearts and bodies as well as to minds. And it evokes, even demands, a response from the congregation to which it is directed.

The preacher as poet has been celebrated by James Weldon Johnson in his poetry cycle, *God's Trombones: Seven Negro Sermons in Verse*. It is in Johnson's preface to this work that we find some of the earliest theorizing about the poetics of the sermon. Preceding his discussion of the preacher's art, Johnson provides a historical look at the preacher's social role as teacher, leader and visionary. His analysis of the preacher's art provides some useful tools for analyzing the art of the poet: "The old-time preacher of parts was above all an orator, and in good measure an actor. He knew the secret of oratory, that at bottom it is a progression of rhythmic words more than it is anything else. . . . He had the power to sweep hearers before him; and so himself was often swept away. At such times his language was not prose but poetry" (5). Johnson goes on to describe this poetic language.

> The old-time Negro preachers . . . were all saturated with the sublime phraseology of the Hebrew prophets and steeped in the idioms of King James English so when they preached and warmed to their work they spoke another language, a language far removed from traditional Negro dialect. It was really a fusion of Negro idioms with Bible English; and in this there may have been, after all, some kinship with the innate grandiloquence of their old African tongues. . . . The old-time Negro preacher loved the sonorous, mouth-filling, ear-filling phrase because it gratified a highly developed sense of sound and rhythm in himself and his hearers. (9)

The elements characteristic of the sermon noted by Johnson in the early part of the twentieth century have persisted in the culture.

Grace Sims Holt, in her essay "Stylin' Outta the Black Pulpit" (in Kochman), points to the traditional church as "an outlet for musical and linguistic expression [in which] a language code emerged to facilitate in-group communication" (190). Holt defines the language practice of the traditional preacher as "stylin' out," a mode of performance in which the preacher will "perform certain acts, say certain things with flourish and finesse" (191). Further, she says, "The rich, descriptive, allegorical phrases in black English are paraded before the congregations and the response of the church is emotionally charged" (196). Bruce Rosenberg, too, notes the "special poetic diction" of the traditional African American preacher, one "derived from his own particular idiomatic dialect of American English . . . specially ordered because of its simplicity, its attention to meter, and its ecclesiastical vocabulary" (101). Such language practice remains commonplace in African American vernacular. It is repeated before small congregations in urban and rural settings weekly, regularly broadcast on the radio, and made available on recordings, most commonly of singing preachers.

There exists in the written tradition, alongside the folk tradition, a poetry of "preachment" (to use Gwendolyn Brooks's term). This poetry in the sermonic mode partakes of the rich and vibrant tradition of the African American folk sermon in form, content, and social purpose. Using language that is both sacred and profane, African American poets within that mode explore the historical experiences of their people, illuminating the past and giving political, social, and moral significance to everyday events. Their poetic reflections on the past are intended for the purposes of present-day enlightenment. These poems illuminate the lessons that can be learned from biblical or historical events. In the words of a common congregational response, poets of preachment "tell the story."

Also, African American poets "make it plain." Their preachments take the reader/ listener to school. Like the preacher, the poets analyze a present reality, explaining the way it is and was, and try to convey answers to such questions as "Why am I treated so bad?" Often such preachments pile up detail upon detail in an effort to elicit congregational assent that the preacher/ poet does indeed understand the reality well enough to be offering instruction or direction. Mari Evans's "Speak the Truth to the People" (*Nightstar*) and Haki Madhubuti's "One-Sided Shoot Out" (*We Walk the Way of the New World*), on the death of Black Panther leader Fred Hampton, are examples of such poems:

> Speak the truth to the people
> Talk sense to the people
> Free them with reason
> Free them with honesty
> Free the people with Love and Courage and Care for
>   their Being
> Spare them the fantasy
> Fantasy enslaves
> A slave is enslaved
> Can be enslaved by unwisdom

Can be enslaved by black unwisdom
Can be re-enslaved while in flight from the enemy
Can be enslaved by his brother whom he loves
His brother whom he trusts
His brother with the loud voice
And the unwisdom

Mari Evans

were the street lights out?
did they darken their faces in combat?
did they remove their shoes to *creep* softer?
could you not see the whi-te of their eyes,
the whi-te of their deathfaces?
didn't yr/look-out man see them coming, coming, coming?
or did they turn into ghostdust and join the night's fog?

Haki Madhubuti

The repetitions and rhythmic structures of these poems enhance their ser-monic character. A call is issued in Evans's repetitions of verbs and Madhubuti's questions. A congregational response of "make it plain" is urged to fill the spaces between the lines. The poets of the New Black Arts movement used the cadences and forms of folk and popular expression. An aesthetics that saw art as functional provided them with an aesthet-ics that included didacticism. This aesthetics of vernacular remains prevalent among African American poets today.

Poetic preachments, like the traditional sermon, offer visions of the future. Inspiration, an exploration of possiblities, an invocation of the way things can be, the ways human beings might be, are some of the modes these preachments take. In a more cautionary vein, there is also the Jere-miad—the warning of judgement that is to come in the last days. When Gwendolyn Brooks preaches in "The Sermon on the Warpland" (in *Blacks*), "Say that the River turns and turn the river," or when Johari Amini warns in her untitled poem "in commemoration of the blk/family" (in *Let's Go Some Where*), "we will be no generashuns to cum for blks r/killing r.selves," prophetic visions and Apocalyptic warnings alike receive the congregational response, "Come on up, now."

It is in the conflation of the roles of the teller of tales and the singer of songs with those of the teacher and preacher that the African American poet becomes the object of the most negative criticism. Under the dictum of the New Criticism that "a poem should not mean but be" and in a critical age when questions of authorial intent are out of fashion, poetic messages are deemed inappropriate. But it is precisely this conflation of roles that is rooted in vernacular culture. The person of words is expected to be a leader or teacher who gives voice and vision to her or his community. "The preacher-poet-performer as creator of social values must tap into [the community's] embedded linguistic code and its attendant responsive mythology if he is to be successful as he *structures* the meaning of blackness" (Hubbard, 10). Preachment or the sermonic mode of discourse influences both structure and theme in African American poetry. Didacticism is an essential element of the texture of language and imagery, and the "language itself creates a vision of an African American perspective toward history" (Hubbard, 18).

An examination of several elegiac poems by Margaret Walker and Gwendolyn Brooks reveals other elements of sermonic language and style. A eulogy is a type of sermon. In the African American tradition, one "speaks well" of the dead so as to inspire the living. Margaret Walker eulogized the slain nationalist leader in "Malcolm X":

> All you violated ones with gentle hearts;
> You violent dreamers whose cries shout heartbreak;
> Whose voices echo clamors of our cool capers,
> And whose black faces have hollowed pits for eyes.
> All you gambling sons and hooked children and bowery bums
> Hating white devils and black bourgeoisie,
> Thumbing your noses at your burning red suns,
> Gather round this coffin and mourn your dying swan.

> Snow-white moslem head-dress around a dead black face!
> Beautiful were your sand-papering words against our skins!
> Our blood and water pour from your flowing wounds.
> You have cut open our breasts and dug scalpels in our brains.
> When and where will another come to take your holy place?
> Old man mumbling in his dotage, or crying child, unborn?

Similarly, Gwendolyn Brooks offered the eulogy "Martin Luther King, Jr."

A man went forth with gifts.
He was a prose poem.
He was a tragic grace.
He was warm music.

He tried to heal the vivid volcanoes.
His ashes are
reading the world.

His Dream still wishes to anoint
the barricades of faith and of control.

His word still burns the center of the sun
above the thousands and the
hundred thousands.

The word was Justice. It was Spoken.

So it shall be spoken.
So it shall be done.

What these two otherwise very dissimilar poems have in common besides their elegiac content is their "preacherly" intent and style. The mode of performance indicated by each poem—that is the speaking style appropriate to the word choice, rhythm, and sense of each poem—evokes the voice of a preacher. Walker's unrhymed sonnet layers on top of its near iambic pentameters the call-and-response rhythms of the folk sermon. The mid-line caesura and ends of each line provide spaces for the congregational response. Similarly, Brooks's shorter free verse lines are punctuated in such a way as to elicit response. Walker's octave-sestet stanzaic pattern provides the poem with its dramatic structure and reinforces its call-and-response pattern. The octave calls the faithful to assemble and mourn "your dying swan." The harshness of the fricatives, sibilants, and aspirates reinforce the poem's violent images. The enumeration of the persons being called to mourn, the "violated ones with gentle hearts" of the poem's first line, are linked with the figure of the first four lines of the sestet—the "dying swan" who wears a "Snow-white moslem head-dress around a dead black face!" The questions of the last two lines of the poem recapitulate the "message" hinted at in the beginning of the sestet. Echoing Yeats and biblical accounts of the crucifixion of Christ, Walker calls her congregation to meditate on the nature of a "savior" and his relationship to his community.

Richard K. Barksdale has linked Walker's use of language to the "orature" of her Jamaican-American preacher father: "Margaret Walker grew up in a household ruled by the power of the word, for undoubtedly few have a greater gift for articulate word power than an educated Jamaican trained to preach the doctrine of salvation in the Black South [where] survival without the mastery of words and language was impossible" (105). Walker's mastery of language is evidenced in usages such as "black bourgeoisie" which is positioned in such a way as to be both an object of the participle "hating" and subject of the participle "thumbing." Her call to "all" to mourn and her closing questions addressed to both the dead Malcolm X and to all who hear or read her poem elicit a congregational response.

D. H. Melhem finds in Brooks's "use of imperatives, parallel constructions and figurative language evoking the Bible" stylistic elements drawn from the tradition of the folk preacher. According to Melhem, "alliteration, epithet, compounding, metaphor, metonymy, and capitalization project a heroic voice spiritually conceived" (1990, 18). The short lines of Brooks's first stanza announce her text and begin the amplification of that text: "A man went forth with gifts." Her repetitive use of "He was " calls the reader as a member of a congregation to reflect on the nature of the man and his gifts and evokes the personage being eulogized, an educated preacher who was a master of the folk style. The lines "His ashes are/reading the world" are an example of the type of startling conceit typical of the sermonic mode. As the poem moves from "His Dream" to "His word," we come to the poem's didactic purpose, its lesson, for "His word still burns." Preacher and poet emerge as parallel figures. Word engenders deed.

The language of both of these elegies is ceremonial. In eulogizing the two fallen leaders, the poets attempt to "make it plain." The poems celebrate the greatness of these heroes, examine the implications of their loss, and affirm hope because of the legacy of these exemplary lives. Like the good funeral sermons that they are, they give comfort and inspiration to those left behind. It is significant that the first book published by Dudley Randall's Broadside Press, almost the official press of the New

Black Arts movement, was an anthology of poems called *For Malcolm* (1969). Established poets such as Gwendolyn Brooks, Margaret Danner, and Robert Hayden share the pages with the emerging writers Conrad Kent Rivers, Jay Wright, Ted Joans, and LeRoi Jones, and even newer voices, such as those of Etheridge Knight, Sonia Sanchez, and Larry Neal. The tradition of African griot is passed on through the folk preacher to the poet.

Two other poems of widely differing styles by Gwendolyn Brooks are illustrative of the ways in which African American poets use the sermonic tradition of the vernacular. The first is "Of DeWitt Williams on his way to Lincoln Cemetery"[1] (from *Blacks*):

> He was born in Alabama.
> He was bred in Illinois.
> He was nothing but a
> Plain black boy.
>
> Swing low swing low sweet sweet chariot.
> Nothing but a plain black boy.
>
> Drive him past the Pool Hall.
> Drive him past the Show.
> Blind within his casket,
> But maybe he will know.
>
> Down through Forty-seventh Street:
> Underneath the L,
> and Northwest Corner, Prairie,
> That he loved so well.
>
> Don't forget the Dance Halls—
> Warwick and Savoy,
> Where he picked his women, where
> He drank his liquid joy,
>
> Born in Alabama.
> Bred in Illinois.
> He was nothing but a
> Plain black boy.

Swing low swing low sweet sweet chariot
Nothing but a plain black boy.

This poem, originally published in *A Street in Bronzeville* (1945), eulo-
gizes by "telling the story" of an apparently brief young life. The folk-
ballad stanzas and spiritual-echoing refrain focus on the details of this
youth's life—where he lived, where he hung out, what he liked to do. In
the repetition of the epithet, "nothing but a plain black boy," the poet as
preacher invests that condition with its own dignity and heroism. This is
a eulogy of comfort. The congregation/ reader is invited to bear witness
to the worth of this life. The poem is addressed directly to a listener/ reader,
and its caesurae and line breaks evoke spoken response. The familiarity
of the refrain hints at communal singing of the funeral service. Taken as
a whole, the poem becomes an exercise in communal remembrance.

The second poem, "The Boy Died in My Alley," also a remembrance
of a dead youth, is more complex. Originally published in 1975 in
Brooks's last volume for Broadside Press, *Beckonings,*² the poem is dedicated "to Running Boy":

The Boy died in my alley
without my Having Known.
Policeman said, next morning,
"Apparently died Alone."

"You heard a shot?" Policeman said.
Shots I hear and Shots I hear.
I never see the Dead.
The Shot that killed him yes I heard
as I heard the Thousand shots before;
careening tinnily down the nights
across my years and arteries.

Policeman pounded on my door.
"Who is it?" "POLICE!" Policeman yelled.
"A Boy was dying in your alley.
A Boy is dead, and in your alley.
And have you known this Boy before"
I have known this Boy before.

I have known this Boy before, who
ornaments my alley.
I never saw his face at all.
I never saw his futurefall.
But I have known this Boy.

I have always heard him deal with death.
I have always heard the shout, the volley.
I have closed my heart-ears late and early.
And I have killed him ever.

I joined the Wild and killed him
with knowledgeable unknowing.
I saw where he was going.
I saw him Crossed. And seeing,
I did not take him down.

He cried not only "Father!"
but "Mother!
Sister!
Brother."
The cry climbed up the alley.
It went up to the wind.
It hung upon the heaven
for a long
stretch-strain of Moment.

The red floor of my alley
is a special speech to me.

The story of this incident is the occasion or text for a sermon on responsibility. The poet/ preacher makes it plain: "We are responsible for our
children." Like Langston Hughes's meditation on a "Junior Addict,"
Brooks's poem is also a lament for a breakdown in community and a call
to action. Through skillful repetition, she continually brings our attention
back to the "Boy"—the unnamed Boy with a capital B whose lonely death
is the central issue, the occasion for the sermon, and the lesson to be learned.
Like any good sermon, the poem builds in intensity. The fifth stanza's rep-

etition of "I have known this Boy" moves us to "And I have killed him ever." When the preacher claims responsibility for the death—worrying the line, though, for two additional stanzas—the broken lines of varying lengths reinforce the strength of emotions displayed and evoked. The cries of "Father!/ . . . Mother!/Sister!/Brother" are the poem's emotional peak, the moment of transformation. Poet/ preacher and reader/ congregation together attain a state of self-knowledge. The sermon summons sinners to the mourners' bench[3] to acknowledge their sins. The closing two lines, "The red floor of my alley/ is a special speech to me," elicit the congregational "Amen."

The lives and deaths of the inhabitants of Gwendolyn Brooks's "Bronzeville," like those of Robert Hayden's Paradise Valley, Langston Hughes's Harlem, or Haki Madhubuti's Chicago, provide the texts for sermonic praises, cautionary warnings, moral and ethical instruction, and prophetic jeremiads. In these communities the everyday and the extraordinary are equally mourned. People like DeWitt Williams and "The Boy" are as significant as Martin Luther King Jr. and Malcolm X.

The poet and the poem are the vehicles through which this important lesson is taught. In the tradition of African praise singing, the subject of the praise-singer's art is asssigned lasting importance. The indivisibility of singing/making poetry and teaching/preaching is one of the marks of African American vernacular culture. Such an assertion does not deny that wordplay, emotional expressiveness, and music are also overarching concerns of the poet's art and craft. Didacticism, however, is assigned an equal value. Not only must a poem *be,* it should *mean.* In the introduction to their 1994 anthology *Every Shut Eye Ain't Asleep,* editors Michael S. Harper and Anthony Walton describe this phenomenon. Much of African American poetry, they assert, has a "historical significance, representing a kind of social, cultural, and political narrative of America, oblique and cubist. Since the beginning blacks have been in the middle of things in America, and [their] poems testify to that reality and celebrate it. Blacks are . . . outsiders at home, and the poems allow for amazing levels of insight within short spaces, what could be called a dialectic of metaphysics and exegesis" (4). The African American poet tells the untold stories, makes plain the other's way of seeing, talking, and being. This literature of social purpose, or preachment, openly offers a canon of personal and group moral and social ethics. It teaches historical, political, and moral lessons. It gives directions for personal and group behavior. It offers explanations for human conduct. Emerging from a context of very specific historical, social, political, and cultural experiences, African American poetry, while always one of the most deeply personal of the expressive arts, reaches outward and addresses its audience.

At their most explicit, African American poets take on the mantle of the biblical prophet Jeremiah, preaching "justice . . . like a mighty stream." Margaret Walker's poem "For My People" is exemplary:

> For my people everywhere singing their slave songs repeatedly:
>   their dirges and their ditties and their blues and jubilees,
>   praying their prayers nightly to an unknown god, bending
>   their knees humbly to an unseen power . . .

Through nine stanzas, each beginning "for my people" or a variant, Walker tells the story of the African American experience in the United States of America. The poem builds in intensity through the accumulation of detail—from childhood through adulthood; from South to North; from rural to urban; at work and at play; past, present, and future. As the poem develops, the implicit congregational responses also build in intensity. As the preacher/poet turns her attention to the future and offers her prophetic vision, we say, "Come on up now," and Walker's peroration concludes:

> Let a new earth rise. Let another world be born. Let a bloody
>   peace be written in the sky. Let a second generation full of
>   courage issue forth; let a people loving freedom come to
>   growth. Let a beauty full of healing and a strength of final
>   clenching be the pulsing in our spirit and our blood. Let the
>   martial songs be written, let the dirges disappear. Let a race
>   of men now rise and take control.

As the poem progresses, its rhythm picks up speed. In the final verse, the pauses come more frequently. The focus of the poem changes from what is or has been to what can be. The final stanza easily lends itself to the singsong chant rhythms of traditional sermonic performance.

The stanza's pattern of accents, its repetitions of dental consonants and blends, and its repetitions of the initial words "Let a" power the stanza forward to its final almost monosyllabic sentence. The poem stands as a model of African American jeremiad. In *The Afro-American Jeremiad: Appeals for Justice in America* (1990), David Howard-Pitney describes this vernacular rhetorical tradition: "The term *jeremiad,* meaning a lamentation or doleful complaint, derives from the Old Testament prophet, Jeremiah, who warned of Israel's fall and the destruction of the Jerusalem temple by Babylonia as punishment for the people's failure to keep the Mosaic covenant. Although Jeremiah denounced Israel's wickedness and foresaw tribulation in the near-term, he also looked forward to the nation's repentance and restoration in a future golden age" (6). Howard-Pitney describes the ways in which African American preachers and orators incorporated this American Protestant tradition into vernacular culture: "As a pervasive idiom for expressing sharp social criticism within normative cultural bounds, the American jeremiad has been frequently adapted for the purposes of black protest and propaganda. . . . Messianic themes of coming social liberation and redemption have deep roots in black culture. . . . The Afro-American jeremiad also expressed black nationalist faith in the missionary destiny of the black race and was a leading instrument of black social assertion in America" (12–13).

In "We Walk the Way of the New World," Haki Madhubuti (formerly Don L. Lee) also assumes the role of a Jeremiah:

> We'll become owners of the   New World
> the New World
> will run it as unowners
> for
> we will live in it too
> & will want to be remembered
> as   real people.

Madhubuti's rhythms are jazzy and percussive as he makes use of the call-and-response impulses of vernacular discourse. In his public readings, Madhubuti uses his poems as texts for a broader lecture or sermon. He assumes his audiences will want to talk back and "say Amen." More recently, Elizabeth Alexander, in her 1994 poem "Narrative: Ali" (in Harper and Walton), exemplifies another way in which poets extend the vernacular tradition of the jeremiad. Subtitled "a poem in 12 rounds," it is a poem sequence of twelve parts that recount in nonlinear fashion the life of prize-fighter Muhammad Ali in his own voice. Alexander's final section is the peroration of a sermon:

> They called me "the fistic pariah."
>
> They said I didn't love my country,
> called me a race-hater, called me out
> of my name, waited for me
> to come out on a street car, shot at me,
> hexed me, cursed me, wished me
> all manner of ill-will,
> told me I was finished.
>
> *Here I am,*
> like the song says,
> *come and take me,*
>
> "The People's Champ,"
>
> myself,
> Muhammad.

Through its use of caesura, repetition, and quotation, the poem dramatically calls attention to the lesson to be learned through the life of its speaker. The poem also illustrates a transcendent moral. The triumph of the heroic victory implicit in the epithet, "The People's Champ," is tied to a process of self-naming, of self-affirmation.

African American poets engage in this same self-naming, self-affirming process. In the many poems about being poets and writing poems, African American poets confront their work, their art, their identity. Gwendolyn Brooks's meditation on the role of the poet found in her book-length poem "Winnie" (1987) elaborates on the preacherly calling of the poet and the relationship of the poem to its audience/readers.

A poem doesn't do everything for you.
You are supposed to go *on* with your thinking.
You are supposed to enrich
the other person's poem with your extensions,
your uniquely personal understandings,
thus making the poem serve *you.*

. . . .

My Poem is life, and is not finished.
It shall never be finished.
My poem is life, and can grow.

. . . .

Nevertheless I put my Poem
which is my life, into your hands, where it will
do the best it can.

Mari Evans offers additional testament to the poet's vocation in her poem "Let Us Be That Something" (*Night Star,* 1981):

If we have the Word let us
say it
If we have the Word let us
Be it
If we have the Word let us
DO
They need something to believe in

This poem is testimony to the power of the word. Implicit in the call to preach, in the religious sense, is the concept of the word as transformative, regenerative, empowering. What can be said can be done. It is in this context, finally, that the centrality of preachment in the African American literary tradition becomes clear. Historically, in African American culture, the person of words has been called upon to play out a social role. Words have been and continue to be weapons used against an entire people. The mastery of the word and the use of language in the struggle for liberation are central. Socially conscious and committed writers not only express themselves but also articulate the experiences and dreams of a people.

"Say that the River turns, and turn the River": words can create new realities. So Langston Hughes could "dream a world" and Amiri Baraka send out, in the poem so-named, an "SOS": "Calling all black people." African American poets, like the evangelists of the traditional church, have been called to proclaim the good news (and the bad). The poetry of preachment represents the enduring vernacular belief in the engendering, empowering word.

CHAPTER 4

Song/Talk

African American Music and Song as Poetic References

*For my people everywhere singing their slave songs
    repeatedly: their dirges and their ditties and their
    blues and jubilees . . .*
MARGARET WALKER

*Come,
let us roam the night together
Singing.*
LANGSTON HUGHES

*we are the hipmen
singing like black doves*
AMUS MOR

Across human cultures, song constitutes the vehicle through which the earliest poets communicated. The debt that African American poetry owes to African American music, including song from the blues and spirituals through jazz, has been discussed by many critics. African American poetry, like much of African American cultural expression, exists in a world of dualities and syncretism. While the Anglo-American poetic tradition has seemed increasingly to move away from orality and music toward abstraction, visual play, and psychological self-probing, poetry of the African world has, often self-consciously, situated itself in a national context, rooted in the particulars of history and culture as much as in individual expression. African American poetry is a product of the complex interplay of cultural marginalization and efforts at cultural self-assertion. African peoples of many traditions enslaved in an alien environment and culture became a new people, forcibly isolated from the mainstream, who lived separately long enough to evolve new and distinct modes of cultural expression. Coming from sophisticated verbal cultures in which oral creativity and musical expression were highly prized, enslaved Wolof, Akan, Yoruba, Kongo, and other people became African Americans, a people with shared cultural values and performance styles.

The forced encounter between the multilingual African and the often monolingual European yielded new forms of these European languages, the pidgins and creoles. Often the linguistic transformations were sound-based. In a recorded lecture on the origins of African American musical traditions, the ethnomusicologist Willis James describes the sounds of the "new" language created by enslaved Africans in the British colonies of North America. The native English speaker might have said, "I am going to go home," contracted at times to "I'm going to go home" or "I'm going home." The African American said and still says, depending on place of origin, circumstance, and meaning, "Ahmo go home," "I'm gonna go home," "Ahm goen home," "I gwine home," or some other variant in pronunciation, rhythm, and pitch. Similarly, the words "come here" can be expressed as "k'mear," "k'meah," "kummear," or "kum hyeah." These sounds generally are not to be found in standard American English but are common in the African American vernacular (James, side 1). They rely on pitch and duration as well as pronunciation to indicate their meaning. Additionally, many words in the English language, such as *goober, okra, gumbo,* and *yam,* have their origins in various African languages.

African American vernacular is not, then, merely a matter of variants in pronunciation and accent alone, but of distinct intonations, durations, and pitches, as well as rhythms—all components of the realm of music. To achieve the particular expressive effects required by a situation, a speaker might commonly add or subtract syllables. "I'm a-gonna walk" replaces "I am going to walk." The song refrain "ain't but me one" expresses the idea that "there isn't anyone left with the exception of me." There is a song, "I got a crown up inna dat Kingdom. Ain't-a dat good news." It would be difficult to capture musically this song's melody and rhythm if one sang it as, "I have a crown up in that kingdom. Isn't that good news." The polyrhythmic demands of African-derived musical expression have also worked their way into American popular culture.

James explores the differences between the chants of African American and white cheerleaders. (The African American style has been mainstreamed considerably in this postsegregation era.) "Rah-rah-rah" or the more British "hip, hip, hurrah" gives way to something like, "We the mighty gents of ole SU/ And we're here to say/ We gon stomp on you// Sing nah, nanananah/ nanananah nananah nananah/ nahnananah." The creation of a verbal artifact, complete with its own particular rhythm, emphasis, tone or pitch, volume or dynamics, and form, is song making. In African American vernacular culture, the performative speech acts of prayer, testimony, and sermon share these characteristic elements of song when they are performed in the singsong style. Observable in services of the traditional church, the singsong style is possibly one of the last vestiges of tonal languages remaining in African American vernacular. In moments of the greatest solemnity and inspiration, pitch and tone become elevated and rhythms regularized. Ceremonial language, phraseology appropriate for announcing the presence of God(s), must be accompanied by appropriate language and sound.

Andrew P. Watson (in C. Johnson, 4)[1] quotes an unidentified worshiper at prayer (the arrangement as verse is mine):

> Lord! Lord! One more kind favor I ask of you.
> Remember the man that is to stand in the gateway
>   and proclaim Your Holy Word.
> Oh, stand by him.
> Strengthen him where he is weak
>   and build him up where he is torn down.
> Oh, let him down into the deep treasures of Your Word.
> And now, O Lord,
> when this your humble servant is done down here
>   in this lowland of sorrow;
> done sitting down and getting up;
> done being called everything
> but a child of God;
> oh, when I am done, done, done,
> and this old world can afford me a home no longer,
> meet me down at the river of Jordan,
> bid the water to be still,
> tuck my little soul away in that snow white chariot,
> and bear it away over yonder
> in the third heaven
> where every day

will be a Sunday,
and my sorrows of this old world
will have an end,
is my prayer
for Christ my Redeemer's sake
and amen
and thank God.

The formulaic language of what is the concluding section of a typical opening prayer of a traditional African American church service would probably be chanted in the "old-timey" or singsong style. The duration of the spondaic call, "Lord! Lord!" is probably equal in chanted length to that of the next four syllables. Each linebreak allows for congregational response and for the supplicant's rhythmic breathing. This style of performance is not a folk tradition in the sense of a vanished oral practice from a distant past. The singsong style is common African American vernacular practice and might be observed and heard any Sunday morning (or Wednesday, Friday, or Saturday evening too) in an African American church. The performative style of the traditional church informs the poetry with a particular kind of musicality that I call song/talk. This inventive use of language displays the performers' pleasure in the sounds and rhythms of the words themselves as well as in the meanings that the words convey. Such poems/songs make use of language that is both functional and ornamental: it is for everyday and for ceremonial use. Song/talk functions in its community telling stories, teaching lessons, preaching sermons, giving praise, pacing the work, tending the children, expressing the feelings that cannot or should not be spoken. Song/talk or lyricism is a sine qua non of African American poetry.

Song/talk manifests itself in several ways. First, the poems themselves usually are musical in their use of sound, language, and rhythm. Also, song and the makers of song are often the subjects of the poems. Finally, song and the makers of song provide a storehouse of referents, metaphor, and allusion for the African American poet. To understand and appreciate African American poetry, it is necessary to know something of the traditions of African American song. The old folks (and some of the young folk, too) do what they call moaning—a kind of humming. As Mari Evans writes in "I Am a Black Woman":

I am a black woman
the music of my song

some sweet arpeggio of tears
is written in a minor key
and I
can be heard humming in the night

Can be heard
          humming
in the night

As a child, I used to hear my great-grandmother "humming in the night." When I first encountered these lines by Mari Evans, the sound of my great-grandmother's voice provided music for Evans's text; it accompanied the musicality inherent in the poet's diction. The nasal and sibilant consonants of "the music of my song/some sweet arpeggio of tears" ripple like musical notes to the repeated onomatopoeic "humming." The poem, which gives its title to the collection, becomes not only a statement of both the communal and universal experience of African American women through history but also a statement of poetic identity and purpose. It is a statement that sings.

Several poems that make use of a superallusive mascon, a figure of great cultural resonance, illustrate the phenomenon of music and song as referent. The metaphor of the river resonates across time in African American musical and poetic traditions. The river appears as a figure in Langston Hughes's "The Negro Speaks of Rivers" (1925), Sterling A. Brown's "Crossing" (c. 1935), and Carolyn M. Rodgers' "How I Got Ovah" (c. 1975). The literal rivers that mark historical experience as well as the figurative ones of the lyrics of the spirituals "Deep River" and "One More River to Cross" provide possible source and subtext for the three poems.

Deep River, my home is over Jordan
Deep River, Lord,
I want to cross over into Camp Ground.
                                Traditional

O wasn't dat a wide river, dat river of Jordan
wide river,
Dere's one more river to cross.
                                Traditional

The spirituals sing of a river and of crossings, of transition from slavery to refuge, home, and freedom. The river is both wide and deep, difficult to cross. The melodies of the two spirituals prolong the words "deep" and "wide." Hughes' use of the word "deep" in his poem resonates with the song "Deep River." The poem's musicality is achieved through long and open vowel sounds combined with liquid, nasal, and sibilant consonants:

> I've known rivers:
> I've known rivers ancient as the world and older than the
>   flow of human blood in human veins.
>
> My soul has grown deep like the rivers.
>
> I bathed in the Euphrates when dawns were young.
> I built my hut near the Congo and it lulled me to sleep.
> I looked upon the Nile and raised the pyramids above it.
> I heard the singing of the Mississippi when Abe Lincoln
>   went down to New Orleans, and I've seen its muddy
>   bosom turn all golden in the sunset.
>
> I've known rivers:
> Ancient dusky rivers.
>
> My soul has grown deep like the rivers.

Making use of common oral figures of repetition, Hughes enumerates rivers associated with African American heritage and history to evoke a mystical sense of the eternal presence of the speaking "I." From the beginnings of recorded history, "the Euphrates"; through the greatness of empire and civilization, "the Nile" and its "pyramids"; through slavery and freedom, "the Mississippi"—the voice proclaims its presence and knowledge, a knowledge not of intellect alone, but of "soul."

Stephen Henderson describes a "metaphysical imagery" as characteristic of African American language style and poetry. Many critics have commented on a strain of mysticism or superstition in African American folk and popular culture. In Hughes's line, "My soul has grown deep like the rivers," the hyperbolic simile resonates on an emotional as well as on an intellectual level. "Deep" is both a physical and a psychic or spiritual measure. The repetition of the first-person pronoun in the context of the poem's statement evokes a communal, racial persona rather than a single individual. The prophetic voice merges with the testifying voice, evidence of the density of the figure of the river.

Sterling A. Brown's "Crossing" speaks of rivers and directly quotes "One More River to Cross." The poem also echoes the song's rhythms:

> This is not Jordan River
> There lies not Canaan
> There is still
> One more wide river to cross
>
> This is the Mississippi
> And the stars tell us only
> That this is not the road

Brown's rivers, however, are rivers of passage and transition, markers of a journey in process with the end not in sight.

> We do not know
> If any have reached that Canaan
> We have received no word
>
> Behind us the belling pack
> Beyond them the hunters
> Before us the dismal swamp.
>
> We do not know. . . .
>
> We have exchanged Louisiana for Mississippi
> Merely
> Georgia for Florida
> Carolina for Tennessee.
>
> We have passed, repassed
> So many rivers
> Okmulgee, Chattahoochee

St Mary's, Mississippi,
Alabama, Tennessee
Mississippi.
We have leapt
From swamp land
Into marshes
We have won through
To bloodred clay
To gravel and rock
To the baked lands
To the scorched barrens.

And we grow footsore
And muscle weary
Our faces grow sullen
And our hearts numb

We do not know . . .
We know only
That there lies not Canaan
That this is no River Jordan.

The poem evokes history through fragments of African American song, images of runaway slaves running from known horrors into unknown terror, and the enumeration of the slave-holding states and the rivers that make up their boundaries and landmarks. In this poem, the rivers are both obstacles and signs of progression or movement. The poet's use of indirection and understatement contributes to the poem's quality of meditation or reflection evoking still another oral genre, the blues. The popular blues theme of travel combines with the escape theme of the spirituals, "Deep river . . . I want to cross over" and "One more river to cross." Even the poem's expressed uncertainty, "We do not know . . ." carries the speaker, this time a communal "we," forward, though the knowledge that, "this is no River Jordan," indicates that this is not a final crossing.

Still are we motherless children
Still are we dragging travelers
Alone, and a long ways from home

> Still with the hard earth for our folding bed
> Still with our head pillowed upon a rock
>
> And still
> With one more river
> Oh, one more wide river to cross.

Brown's incorporation of phrases from traditional songs, "motherless children," "dragging travelers," "a long ways from home," exemplifies still another vernacular practice, a kind of borrowing or quotation that in its latest version is the electronic "sampling" of rap music. The re-creative process lends value. This combining of fragments from other works, not necessarily one's own, is more than simple allusion. The verbal pastiche incorporates a multiplicity of meanings that separately and together work to enrich the poem as a whole. The final "wide river" of the poem is illustrative. Just as the spirituals encoded secular messages in spiritual texts, this poem offers both literal and historical meanings as well as metaphorical ones. In the mode of "I say this to say that," Brown embeds in his poetic rememberings of past crossings and songs/poems about crossings a meditation on life's final crossing. The historical, literary, and folk associations of death with the crossing of a river are given racial expression by a poet who embeds his metaphor in African American vernacular song.

For Carolyn Rodgers, fifty years after Hughes and forty years after Brown, the river retains its associative power both musically and metaphorically. By this time, the popular song, "River's Invitation," might also serve as source. That song sings of the seductive temptation to suicide by drowning. Other gospel songs sing of the healing and regenerative powers of holy rivers. Most certainly Rodgers was aware of the songs and Hughes's text, and possibly those of other poets who used this figure, when she wrote "How I Got Ovah":

> i can tell you
> about them
> i have shaken rivers
> out of my eyes
> i have waded eyelash deep
> have crossed rivers

> have shaken the water weeds out
> of my lungs
> have swam for strength
> through waterfalls with electric beats
> i have bore the shocks
> of water deep deep
> waterlogs are my bones
> i have shaken the water free of my hair
> have kneeled on the banks
> and kissed my ancestors of the dirt
> whose rich dark roots fingers rose up reached out
> grabbed and pulled me rocked me capped me
> gentle strong and firm
> carried me
> made me swim for strength
> cross rivers
> though i shivered
> was wet with cold
> and wanted to sink down
> and float as water, yea—
> i can tell you
> i have shaken rivers
> out of my eyes.

The references to crossing rivers and the "water deep deep" call up both the spirituals and the Hughes poem, and like them, it sings. Rodgers gives the poem (and volume) the title of an old gospel hymn, illustrating the way in which African American poets turn to music as a source for meanings and images. The poem and song share meaning in their explorations of the way in which the gospel singer and poet have successfully traversed the river(s) of life. As the spiritual identifies the biblical Jordan with the river of life, Sterling Brown and Carolyn Rodgers recognize that life has many crossings. Rodgers's poem resonates with the texts of Brown and Hughes as well as the spirituals, gospel song, and popular song alluded to by her title and text.

The crossings of rivers evoke still another major musical leitmotif or mascon of African American poetry—the train. African American music proliferates with journeys and means of journeying. The ships of the middle passage were transformed in African American song into the "Ship of Zion" which could carry one home. Biblical texts also offered another means of transport, the chariot. By the nineteenth century, African American reality included the train. The spiritual exhorted the slaves to "Get on Board" the Gospel Train. They named their physical escape route from slavery to freedom the Underground Railroad, and Robert Hayden, in his masterwork "Runagate Runagate," has Harriet Tubman sound the call to "come ride-a my train" across the ages. In the postslavery era, one of African American song's greatest heroes was the railroad worker John Henry, whose story was retold by several poets, including Margaret Walker. The train provides the blues singer with the favored mode of escape. "When a man gets the blues/ He grabs a train and rides."

That a musician by the name of John Coltrane should emerge as cultural icon in the 1960s was an occasion of literary serendipity. The body of poems about trains and "Trane" could constitute its own anthology. Coltrane moves through the poems of the New Black Arts movement. Haki Madhubuti dedicated his second book to John Coltrane as well as the title poem of his third book, *Don't Cry Scream* (1969). Sonia Sanchez's "a/coltrane/poem," Askia Muhammad Toure's "Juju," and Carolyn M. Rodgers's "Me, in Kulu Se and Karma" celebrate particular Coltrane recordings. Michael S. Harper's *Dear John, Dear Coltrane,* his first publication, is replete with Coltranesque explorations, as is his 1985 volume, *Healing Song for the Inner Ear.* In a 1981 interview Harper described the relationship of his poetry to the music: "Blacks have always infused the language with elegance and with word invention as an improvisational attitude; I grew up making words, describing events, often hostile to me, in a kind of operatic parody. . . . We loved the musicians for their artistry and their elan, and we learned their coded phrasings" (94).

Jazz and jazz-influenced poetry are, of course, children of the blues. At the heart of jazz is improvisation. African American poets imply improvisation in their texts, in part through punctuation or its absence, as in Johari Amini's untitled poem "in commemoration of the blk/family." The poem rushes to its mournful conclusion "we will be no more" with only an occasional line-space or slash as punctuation. Additionally, a poem in performance often differs from the published version. From jazz vocalists, the poet appropriates scatting, making musical and rhythmic wordless sounds. Aldon Nielsen points out the "thin line between song and speech . . . between the written and the oral . . . so thin as to render any opposition between the two insupportable" (218). The soundings of the text, then, are the equivalent of music. Both African American poets and musicians have recognized interrelationship between their arts. Archie Shepp,[2] a prominent jazz saxophone player, "typically viewed aesthetic issues in terms of a continuum between music and literature, often . . . employing an analogy from one art form to elucidate another" (Nielsen, 181). Jayne Cortez is one of the poets who write out of a jazz tradition. She takes the Duke Ellington title, "The Drum Is a Woman," and riffs[3] on the metaphor as one for abuse by a spouse or lover: "If the drum is a woman/ why are you pounding your drum into an insane/ babble." In such poems as "I See Chano Pozo," Cortez is so musical that her solo performances "seem to be written as a capella music" (Nielsen, 221). (She also often performs with percussion and other jazz accompaniment.) As Etheridge Knight has written, in an untitled haiku (no. 9):

> Making jazz swing in
> Seventeen syllables AIN'T
> No square poet's job.

The blues tradition provides other contributions to song/talk. The blues is a musical form, a stanzaic pattern, an attitude, and an ethos or way of life. Langston Hughes and Sterling Brown, in the ambience of the race-conscious Harlem Renaissance, found poetic inspiration in blues singers and musicians as well as in the music and its form. From *The Weary Blues* (1926) to *The Panther and the Lash* (1967), Hughes explored myriad permutations of the blues:

> Homesick blues, Lawd
> 'S a terrible thing to have.
> Homesick blues is
> A terrible thing to have.
> To keep from cryin'
> I opens ma mouth an' laughs.
>   "Homesick Blues"

> Sun's a risin'
> This is gonna be ma song

I could be blue but
I been blue all night long.
                    "Hey! Hey!"

Beats ma wife an'
Beats ma side gal too
Don't know why I do it
It keeps me from feelin' blue
                    "Bad Man"

Tell me, Mister Backlash,
What do you think I got to lose?
I'm gonna leave you, Mister Backlash,
Singing your mean old backlash blues.
                    "Backlash Blues"

Hughes's blues stanzas, to a greater or lesser degree, fit the twelve-bar musical pattern that constitutes the blues form. Hughes also recognizes, however, that the blues is more than a form. "Still Here" captures the blues ethos:

I've been scared and battered
My Hopes the wind done scattered.
Snow has friz me, sun has baked me.
Looks like between 'em
They done tried to make me
Stop laughin', stop lovin', stop livin'—
But I don't care!
I'm still here!

The personal "I" articulates the experience of the communal-racial "we." As Sherley Anne Williams has observed, "individual experience plays against the assumed knowledge of collective history in much the same way that the communal pattern of call and response plays against the individual experience expressed in the blues" (84). Sterling Brown's praise poem "Ma Rainey" describes this relationship between the blues performer and her audience: "Git way inside us,/ Keep us strong. . . . " Brown goes on to narrate one man's description of Rainey's performance of "The Backwater Blues"—"She jes' catch hold of us, somekindaway"—and directly quotes from "The Backwater Blues."

In the African American vernacular tradition, the blues functions as both narrative and lyric song. It is a mode of narrative of personal experience that is also expressive of personal philosophy and emotion. At the same time, the blues audience testifies to or affirms the universal truth and applicability of the singer and her song. Albert Murray has described the varied ways in which the blues idiom is "survival technique, aesthetic equipment for living and a central element in the dynamics of U.S. Negro life style" (*Omni-Americans,* 58). He explores this ethos in greater detail in his volume *Stomping the Blues* (1976) as a "disposition to encounter obstacle after obstacle as a matter of course . . . an exercise in heroic action (254)."

Examining that most common of blues themes, romance gone wrong—"The blues ain't nothin/ but a woman cryin for her man"—we may glimpse some of the ways in which poets extend the blues tradition. In 1969 the songwriter Val Gray Ward sang in "Val's Blues":

> The day you walked away and left me
> You didn't even say goodbye.
> I hung my head down in sorrow
> All I could do was cry
> You broke my heart,
> Darling, you broke my heart.
>
> I keep answering the doorbell
> That doesn't even ring
> I take the receiver off my telephone
> I cannot hear a thing.
> You broke my heart,
> Darling, you broke my heart.

Ward is using a variant of the traditional blues stanza that alternates a long rhymed couplet with a refrain. Her sentiment is commonplace. In the same vein, in "Where Have You Gone" (from *I Am a Black Woman*), Mari Evans writes:

> Where have you gone . . .
> with your confident

walk . . . with
your crooked smile . . .

why did you leave
me
when you took your
laughter
and departed
Are you aware that
with you
went the sun
all light
and what few stars
there were? . . .
Where have you gone
with your confident
walk your
crooked smile the

rent money
in one pocket and
my heart
in another . . .

The hard reality of the lover who absconds with both the rent money and her heart is the reality of the blues singers of Robert Hayden's "Homage to the Empress of the Blues" and Gwendolyn Brooks's "Queen of the Blues." It is worth noting that Hayden's poem has a presumably male speaker hypothesizing the cause of the Empress's song, whereas Brooks's Queen, with very little narrative interpolation, speaks for herself.

Judith Simmons captures not only the form and language of the blues idiom but some of its indomitable spirit in "Judith's Blues":

git it on heaven,
git it on
git it on, God,
let it rain

let it fall like it fell on Noah
let it wash away all my pain

git it on, cloud,
git it on
git it on, thunder
hear yo roar
let the lightnin flash
up and down the sky
git it on, Jesus, baby, git it on

when I woke up this mornin
I started listenin to the blues

shoulda stayed in bed with my eyes shut tight
cause today's just like old news, all used

all I know ain nothin gonna happen
that ain happening befo
so git it on, Big father, laying up in the sky
git it on, Sweet Jesus, let it po

The "vamping" rhythm of the third stanza reminds us of Murray's assertion that the blues is a "never-ending sequence of escapades" (*Stomping*, 254). Additionally, the poet "cops" a blues attitude. It is the defiant stance of her lyric as well as its musicality that comprise the song/talk of "Judith's Blues."

The traditional "How Long Blues"—

If I could holler like a mountain jack
I'd go up the mountain, call my baby back
How long, how long, tell me, baby, how long

—echoes in "Feeling Fucked Up," Etheridge Knight's blues:

Lord she's done gone left me done packed / up and split
and I with no way to make her

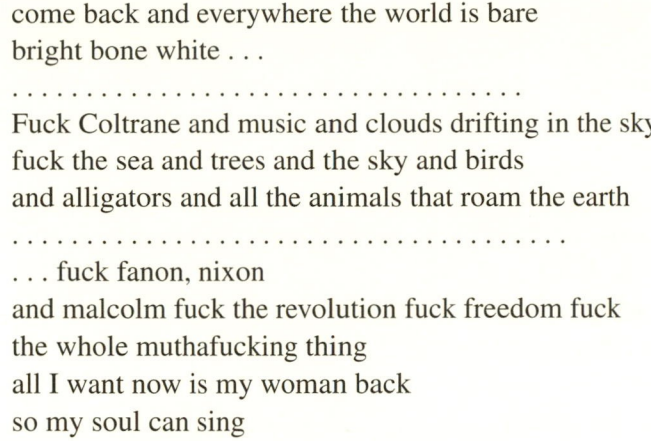

come back and everywhere the world is bare
bright bone white . . .

. . . .

Fuck Coltrane and music and clouds drifting in the sky
fuck the sea and trees and the sky and birds
and alligators and all the animals that roam the earth

. . . .

. . . fuck fanon, nixon
and malcolm fuck the revolution fuck freedom fuck
the whole muthafucking thing
all I want now is my woman back
so my soul can sing

Knight's poem laments a lost love in the language of the streets, essentially worrying the line that might be said to summarize one aspect of the blues ethos. The hypermasculinity of the poem's profanity stands in tension with the vulnerability expressed by the disappointed bluesman persona. Perhaps the bluesman must be profane in order to be tender. (I explore black poets' uses of profanity at greater length in chapter 5.) As Knight's rejected lover dismisses everything one might consider important in the world, he reaches a point where he runs out of words and culminates his profane litany with "the whole muthafucking thing." His blues-tinged climactic lines, "all I want now is my woman back/ so my soul can sing," provide a release of the tension built up in his audience or readers. The repetitions of the second stanza, with its mixture of objects enclosed in a poem that begins with "Lord she's gone" and ends with "all I want now is my woman back," bespeak the poet's skillful choice of oral idioms in which to voice his blues. The poem is both blues and street rant and, ultimately, a very personal lyric song.

The distance between blues and gospel music is not great. Thomas A. Dorsey, known as the Father of Gospel Music, began his musical career as Georgia Tom, a blues pianist and composer. One example illustrates the multiplicity of ways in which African American poets incorporate both sacred and secular song traditions within the same poem. Gwendolyn Brooks's "Infirm"[4] (from *Blacks*) evokes that aspect of the gospel tradition that has often caused gospel music to be described as "the holy blues":

Everybody here
is infirm.
Everybody here is infirm.
Oh mend me. Mend me. Lord.

Today I
say to them
say to them, Lord
Look! I am beautiful, beautiful with
my wing that is wounded
my eye that is bonded
or my ear not funded
or my walk all a-wobble
I'm enough to be beautiful.

You are
beautiful too.

Brooks's first stanza has a pattern similar to the stanzaic pattern or structure of the traditional blues lyric. But as the poet, like the blues singer, calls on the "Lord" to hear the poem's cry, gospel, too, is evoked. Just as contemporary gospel music often blurs the line between the sacred and profane by simply substituting "the Lord" for "my baby" in popular songs of the day, the contemporary African American poet extols the profane in sacred terms and discusses the sacred in profane terms. Brooks plays prayerlike words against blues rhythms in the manner of gospel song. Her vamping rhythm in the second stanza begs for instrumental response as it builds to the affirming climactic line, "I'm enough to be beautiful." The final stanza of the poem, through the arrangement of its four words on the page, marries sound and rhythm to sense in the manner of song.

When music and its makers become the subjects of the poet's art, artistic politics usually come into play. The Paul Laurence Dunbar poem "When Malindy Sings" (c. 1895) is illustrative:

G'way an' quit dat noise, Miss Lucy—
    Put dat music book away;
What's de use to keep on tryin'?
    Ef you practice twel you're gray,

You cain't sta't no notes a-flyin'
    Lak de ones dat rants and rings
From the kitchen to de big woods
    When Malindy sings.

Like many works by Dunbar and other African American poets, "When Malindy Sings" has been set to music,[5] testimony to its inherent lyricism. Additionally, this poem is one of many that sing the praises of a particular musician. Malindy's artistry is of a superior order in its power to give pleasure to her listeners. It also, for the poem's speaker, is evidence of the superiority of African American talent over white training.

African American poetry has long acknowledged its debt to song and songmakers. (The Western poetic convention that recognizes poetry's oral origins through invocations to the poetic muse might be considered another source of this aspect of the vernacular tradition.) The unknown creators of the spirituals are praised by such poets as James Weldon Johnson (in the 1935 poem "O Black and Unknown Bards," in *St. Peter Relates an Incident*) and Lance Jeffers (in the 1974 poem "On Listening to the Spirituals," in *When I Know the Power of My Black Hand*). Poets from Langston Hughes, with his celebrations of the be-boppers in the forties, through Ted Joans and Bob Kaufman's Beat Era tributes to jazz musicians in the fifties and sixties, to contemporary celebrations of the music and its performers by such artists as Jayne Cortez and Ntozake Shange recognize African American music both as aesthetic source and measure for poetic aspirations. In this poetry, Lightnin Hopkins, Howling Wolf, Muddy Waters, and Memphis Slim (their names are song/talk) become icons. The praise names—Duke, Count, Prez, and Bird—and the first names needing no further identification—Bessie, Mahalia, Billie, Dinah, Aretha[6]—are scattered throughout the pages of any anthology of African American poetry one might open.

Rhythm and blues and later forms of popular music offer their own particular iconographies as well. Nikki Giovanni's 1970 poem "Revolutionary Dreams" (from *Re: Creation*) depends for its meaning on the reader's familiarity with the Raelets and the Sweet Inspirations, back-up singers during the 1960s for Ray Charles and Aretha Franklin, respectively:

In my younger years
. . . .

> I wanted to be
> a raelet
> and say "dr o wn d in my youn tears"
> or "tal kin bout tal kin bout"
> . . . .
> then as I grew and matured
> I became more sensible
> and decided I would
> settle down
> and just become
> a sweet inspiration

If the reader is also familiar with the songs being quoted and knows that the phrase "sweet inspiration" might also allude to a song title, the poem's meaning is further illuminated. The metaphor of "The Black Back-Ups," the title poem of Kate Rushin's 1980s collection, once again is understandable if the reader recognizes even a few of the names mentioned in the poem's opening lines. The poet invokes them as a way to celebrate ordinary African American working women. This is dedicated to Merry Clayton, Fontella Bass, Vonetta

> This is dedicated to Merry Clayton, Fontella Bass, Vonetta Washington,
> Carolyn Franklyn, Yolanda McCullough,
> Carolyn Willis, Gwen Guthrie, Helaine Harris, and Darlene
> Love. This is for all of the Black women who sang back-up for
> Elvis Presley, John Denver, James Taylor, Lou Reed.
> Etc. Etc. Etc.

The language of African American music informs the language of African American poetry. "When musicians say cookin/ it is food for the soul/ that is being prepared . . ." (Baraka/Jones, "I Am Speaking of Future Good-ness and Social Philosophy," in *Black Magic*). Song functions in African American vernacular culture as primary recorder, the means of documentation of life and experience. Making music, then, continuing the song/talk that records and passes on the story, documents the events, celebrates the heroes, exposes the evils, and exhorts the people to keep on keeping on is the mission of the poet as well. The contemporary African American poet sings to a community and from a vibrant oral tradition by making song/talk.

Tell My Story

Boast and Toast Traditions

I'm a Man . . .
> **Bo Diddley**

I'm a Woman . . .
> **KoKo Taylor**

The magic words are:
> **Amiri Baraka**

here u are actin not like decent folks
> *talkin bout hatin white folks & revolution*
& such and runnin round wid NegroEs
> *WHO CURSE IN PUBLIC!!!!*
> **Carolyn Rodgers**

My discussion of voice in poetry concentrated on the dramatic and performative effects of the poetic uses of the first person. This chapter
examines in greater detail the self-affirming voice and the narrative
voice. The self-affirming voice is the most individual and personal, the
least communal of the poetic stances. Its annunciatory "I am" demands
no communal assent. Rather, the desired response is most often admira-
tion. Frequently such statements also draw attention to the speaker's linguistic prowess. This assertive voice in much of African American poetry
has strong vernacular roots in the boast, a genre of poetry from urban street
culture in which young men, in the most hyperbolic manner, affirm their
worth in terms of physical strength, sexual prowess, and the ability to inflict
harm. The boast is an almost exclusively male style of performance in
its vernacular manifestations. In my youth I frequently heard young
men reciting these often scatological rhymes. The performances placed

emphasis on the rhythms, rhymes, and often profane wordplay. Although I do not recall an instance of a young girl reciting a similar poem, I recognize today that some of the jump-rope rhymes and other girls' games contained similar rhymes.[1] While a girl might toss off an occasional self-praising couplet, I never heard one go on at the length of, say, "Rap's Poem" (cited in chapter 2).

In style and subject these rhymes closely resemble one strain of the blues. In a 1967 essay, "I Can Peep through Muddy Water & Spy Dry Land: Boasts in the Blues" (in Dundes), Mimi Clar Melnick explores the ways in which the blues boast functions in vernacular culture: "in the cleverest possible language, the blues singer dreams of personal greatness . . . brags of his accomplishments, and in no uncertain terms establishes himself as a hero. . . . His boasts provide him with an outlet for his aggressions and frustrations, lend him a means for expressions of protest, and are generally designed to help him *be somebody* with the greatest style and color" (268).

The 1950s blues songs "I'm a Man," composed and performed by Bo Diddley, and "I'm Your Hoochie Coochie Man," composed by Willie Dixon for performance by Muddy Waters, are musical relatives of the boast, as is their later 1980s relative "I'm a Woman," composed and sung by Koko Taylor. (The fairly late appearance of the Taylor lyric is perhaps an indication of how recently it has become socially acceptable in the United States for women to boast in public and for African American women to do so in an interracial sphere.[2] What the three blues songs do is to affirm the singer's existence in the world as a self-defining human being.

> Now when I was a little boy, At the age of five,
> I had somethin' in my pocket, Keep a lot o' folks alive.
>
> NOW I'M A MAN, Made twenty-one,
> You know, baby, We can have a lot o' fun
>
> All you pretty women stand in line,
> I can make love to you, baby, in an hour's time.
>
> I'm goin' back to Kansas soon,
> Bringin' back a second cousin, Little John the Conkeroo.

The line I shoot would never miss,
The way I make love to 'em, they can't resist

> Bo Diddley, "I'm a Man"

The gypsy woman told my mother, before I was born,
You got a boy-child coming, he's gonna be a son-of-a-gun
He's gonna make pretty women, he's gonna make 'em jump and
    shout
Then the world could know what this was all about

Lord, I'm here, oh yeah
Everybody knows I'm here, oh Lord,
'Cause I'm a Hoochie Coochie Man
Everybody knows I'm here.

I got a black cat's bone, I got a mojo too,
I'm John the Conqueror, I'm gonna mess with you.
I'm gonna make your pretty girls lead me by the hand,
Then the world will know I'm the hoochie coochie man

On the seventh hour, and on the seventh day
On the seventh month, the seven doctors say
He was born for good luck and that you're gonna see,
I've got seven hundred dollars, baby, don't you mess with me

> Willie Dixon, "I'm Your Hoochie
> Coochie Man"

When I was a little girl, only twelve years old
I couldn't do nothing to save my doggone soul
My mama told me the day I was grown
She said, sing the blues, child, sing it from now on

I'm a Woman, oh yeah, I'm a ball of fire
I'm a Woman; I can make love to a crocodile
I'm a Woman; I can sing the blues
I'm a Woman; I can change old to new
Spell W-O-M-A-N, oh yeah, that means I'm grown

I'm a Woman; I'm a rushing wind
I'm a Woman; can cut stone with a pin
I'm a Woman; I'm a love maker
I'm a Woman; you know I'm a earthshaker

I'm a Woman; I know my stuff
I'm a Woman; I ain never had enough

I'm going down yonder behind the sun
I'm gon do something for you ain never been done
I'm gon hold back the lightnin with the palm of my hand
Shake hands with the devil, make him crawl in the sand
       I'm a Woman . . .
             Koko Taylor, "I'm a Woman"

The lyrics affirm the singers most specifically as sexual beings. The language is more explicit than the lyrics of many country blues artists or the double-entendres of the more widely known classic blues artists from the turn of the century up through the twenties and thirties, such as Ma Rainey and Bessie Smith, but the sentiment is the same. The indirection of figures such as "Rock me all night long" or "I want a little sugar in my bowl" might be a little too subtle for the mid- through late-twentieth-century audience. The language of these lyrics, however, shares with those of folk blues such elements as an emphasis on the physical and a blurring of distinction between the figurative and the literal.

In his 1973 study, "The Country Blues as Meaning," Stephen Calt points out the conversational tone of blues lyrics, the colloquial nature of the metaphors and similes, and the widespread use of concrete nouns. That Bo Diddley, Willie Dixon, and Koko Taylor all articulate identity in terms of sexual power places them solidly in a vernacular tradition that seeks to disempower the stereotype of African American hypersexuality through appropriation. Their lyrics, however, also merely follow the stylistic and figurative conventions of a genre. Similarly, today when rap music by men uses language of a highly sexualized masculinity, female rappers such as Little Kim identify female power in equally crude terms. Cultural ambivalence about acceptable roles for women is reflected in the music and in the poetry.[3]

Out of such blues boasts or alongside of them (I posit neither chronology nor causality) comes the urban contemporary vernacular language situation of "rappin." Rappin is the name for the inventive language acts originally used primarily by young African American men in their self-introductions or in their approaches to young women. Very often rhymed, these self-introductions echo traditional African warriors' boasts designed to intimidate potential enemies into not issuing a challenge. This form of oral poetry is common in many cultures. However, African American men have implanted this tradition into the vernacular. I believe this form is a cultural retention, commonplace enough in Africa to have survived in the New World. In his anthology *Understanding the New Black Poetry,* Stephen Henderson includes an example of this art from H. Rap Brown's autobiography, *Die Nigger Die.* Brown's verbal skills were the source of his name "Rap."

I'm sweet peeter jeeter the woman beater
The baby maker the cradle shaker
The deerslayer the buckbinder the woman finder
Known from the Gold Coast to the rocky shores of Maine
Rap is my name and love is my game.

The relationship in language, style, and attitude between such a rhyme and the earlier cited blues lyrics is clear. Sexual prowess again is the basis of identity and affirmation. While the sweet-talking, seductive rapper has earned his own place in African American folklore, the term has evolved more recently in popular culture to describe all the boasting, bragging, assertive oral chants that are now an established part of the recording industry in the United States. Rappin's use of hyperbole, virtuoso rhyming, tropes, and the varying rhythms of African American music are turned into poetry in a multiplicity of ways. Poets use the rhythms, figures, and attitudes of the vernacular rapper. Larry Neal was certainly aware in 1967 of the multiple references to the seventh son in vernacular blues culture and folklore when he gave voice to Malcolm X; Ishmael Reed combines a scenario from the cowboy movies of American popular culture, the mythology of ancient Egypt, and African American popular dance; amd Mari Evans recites historical fact in such a way as to render her speaker heroic, even mythic.

I am the Seventh Son of the son
who was also the seventh.
I have drunk deep of the waters of my ancestors,
have traveled the soul's journey toward cosmic harmony—
the Seventh Son.

> Larry Neal, "Malcolm X—An Autobiography"

I am a cowboy in the boat of Ra. I bedded
down with Isis, Lady of the Boogaloo, dove
down deep in her horny, stuck up her Wells-Far-ago
in daring midday getaway.

> Ishmael Reed, "I Am a
> Cowboy in the Boat of Ra"

I have wrested wheat fields
from the forests
turned rivers
from their courses
leveled mountains
at a word
festooned the land with
bridges
> gemlike
on filaments of steel
> moved
glistening towersofBabel in place
> like blocks
sweated a whole
civilization

> Mari Evans, "Vive Noir"

The voices in these poems come to life, in part, through their vernacular assocations. What the poets do, however, is expand the basis on which their speakers affirm selfhood. Nikki Giovanni's "Ego Tripping" (in *Re: Creation*) is another example of poetic boast as she gives voice to "Mother" Africa: "I was born in the Congo." The African American poet turns the boast into a poetry of affirmation. Written by male and female poets alike, these poems affirm the individual's existence in the world on his or her own terms. The poetic voice may be a personal one, or it may articulate a communal assertion. The poet also may choose to give voice to an obvious other.

Participation in this tradition is not restricted to poetry of the New Black Arts era. The following lines by Langston Hughes and Margaret Walker, from the 1920s and 1970s respectively, share elements of structure, rhythm, and attitude with the boast tradition.

> I am a Negro:
>> Black as the night is black,
>> Black like the depths of my Africa.
>>> Langston Hughes, "Negro"

> I'm Harriet Tubman, people,
> I'm Harriet the slave,
> I'm Harriet, free woman,
> And I'm free within my grave.
>
> I killed the overseer.
> I fooled old marster's eyes,
> I found my way to Canada
> With hundreds more besides.
>> Margaret Walker,
>> "Harriet Tubman"

Hughes's speaker, like those in the poems by Evans and Giovanni, affirms existence and claims power through heritage and by a history of work and achievement from Africa to the United States. Walker's Tubman, on the other hand, tells her story in the matter-of-fact language appropriate to a ballad. She affirms her self-making in her progression from slavery to freedom. Walker and Hughes in their poems play off the rhythms, and in Walker's case, rhymes, of the vernacular boast. The poems are evidence of their makers' expanding definitions of self, manhood, and womanhood.

The blues ethos in African American vernacular culture also manifests itself in another form of expressive or performance culture, the toast. S. H. Fernando, in his 1994 study of hip-hop culture, describes the toast as "folk poetry from the underbelly of society" (84). These narrative poems from African American oral tradition celebrate the exploits of "bad" men like Stagger Lee and Dolomite, tricksters like the Signifyin Monkey, and other outsiders such as pimps or Shine, the only African American on the *Titanic*.[4] Roger Abrahams (1970) and Bruce Jackson (1974) have compiled collections of the texts of many of these folk poems. Jackson has also compiled field recordings of some classic toasts (see the discography). The folk blues and ballads, too, about heroic figures like John Henry and the "badman" Stagger Lee as well as blues songs like "All Night Long" (composed by Willie Dixon for performance by Koko Taylor) are musical relatives of such toasts. Renditions of the exploits of the Signifyin Monkey, Shine, Dolomite, and the Hustlers' Convention or Ball were commonplace enough that cleaned-up versions made their way into popular commercial recordings such as Nat King Cole's 1940s hit "Straighten Up and Fly Right," Oscar Brown Jr.'s 1960s "Signifyin Monkey," and The Last Poets' 1970s "Hustler's Convention." Only Shine resisted taming until Etheridge Knight and Larry Neal wrestled him into poetry in such works as Knight's "Dark Prophecy: I Sing of Shine" (49) and Neal's poetic monologues in the voice of Shine, all published during the nineteen-seventies.

In his discussion of the toast, Bruce Jackson identifies its most common themes as "violence, sex, and the failure of romance" (12). He further points out that while it "is easy to see the street roles portrayed in the toasts as models for street youths, . . . they are also terribly threatening to them: the badman will beat you up; the pimp will hustle your sister or your mother or your woman; the pusher will sell a product other people rob you to buy; the hustler will take your money" (15). It is in this contradictory space that the "ghetto cautionary tale" becomes a major genre. Amiri Baraka's poem "Black People" (c. 1965, in his *Selected Poetry*) uses incendiary language (so much so that it was cited as a reason for jailing him as a dangerous person) to voice African American grievances and rage in language we have grown accustomed to in this age of gangsta rap.

> . . . Money don't grow on trees no
> way, only whitey's got it, makes it with a machine, to control you
> you cant steal nothin from a white man, he already stole it he owes
> you anything you want, even his life. All the stores will open if you

> will say the magic words. The magic words are: Up against the
> wall mother fucker this is a stick up!

Equally shocking at the time, Nikki Giovanni's 1968 poem "The True
Import of Present Dialogue Black vs. Negro" (in *Black Feeling, Black Talk*)
rhetorically asked, "Nigger/ can you kill." Like boasts and toasts, this type
of poem provides its readers with a vicarious sense of power, a way of
affirming self in the world. It is not, however, necessarily prescriptive.
Langston Hughes's "Junior Addict" and Johari Amini's "A Revolutionary Requiem in Five Parts," as well as Baraka's "Bad News for Your High-
ness/(Song to Deposed Kings)," all written between 1965 and 1970,
describe the waste of lives lived in servitude to a drug habit. (These poems
in their treatment of the 1960s heroin epidemic can be compared with contemporary poetic responses to today's crack cocaine epidemic.) Just as
the vernacular outlaws Stagger Lee and Dolomite are likely to end up in
jail or dead in hell, African American poetry's outlaws, too, most often
come to no-good ends.

Greg Tate has recognized the role played by the New Black Arts movement in the generation of rap culture when he posits Amiri Baraka as a
father of rap. Tate notes Baraka's "genius at crystallizing the Northern
urban African American male experience—his gifts for making prose poetry
out of the body of cultural attitudes toward music, speech, style, and women
which bind and shape big city brothers" (174). In his poetry of the Black
Arts era, Baraka turned to African American popular culture and the "language of the streets" to give vitality and racial authenticity to his art. Such
poems as "20th-Century Fox" and "Lady Bug" (both in his *Selected Poetry*),
originally published in the late 1960s, make use of the jump rope and children's rhyme rhythms of the boast as well as profane language to create
what Henderson has termed a "verbalized social dissonance" (41). Vernacular uses of profane language call attention to the disjuncture between
social situation and vocabulary with humorous, defensive, or aggressive
effect. In the late sixties African American poets began using this technique with dramatic impact, as in Madhubuti's toastlike poem, "A Rev-
olu-tionary Screw" (in *Directionscore*).

The defiant stance and valorizing of outlaws inherent in the toast tradition is evident in the language choices of the New Black Arts movement. The widespread use of "nigger" and "motherfucker" is one of the
hallmarks of the age. I would argue, however, that in this case the liter-

ary practice in some ways drove the vernacular practice more than the reverse. The impact of published writers standing up on platforms and cussing in public has not been examined to date. The avowed intent of the writers was to speak in the "language of the people." They claimed revolutionary purpose and authenticated lumpen credentials in an anti-establishment age. Writers like Etheridge Knight, an actual recovering drug addict and exconvict, and the children of the bourgeoisie like Amiri Baraka alike engaged in this discourse. Throughout the sixties and seventies, there was discussion about the appropriateness and validity of this language practice. As Henderson notes, there was a danger that the terminology would be used crudely, too liberally, and for shock value only.

In the most effective usages, however, the words functioned as mascons of tremendous power, as in the previously cited Baraka poem "Black People!" Criticism of the language of the New Black Arts poets was based both in generational and class bias, although white critics voiced their objections in aesthetic terms. The poets' responses were often humorous. Just as Carolyn Rodgers was moved to write "The Last M. F." in 1969 (in *Songs of a Black Bird*), Mona Lisa Saloy in 1994 published "The 'N' Word," which she dedicated to Carolyn Rodgers. "They tell me," Saloy writes, "I shouldn't use/ The 'N' word in the 90's." Rodgers concludes:

> and so i say
> this is the last poem i will write calling
> all manner of wites, card-carrying muthafuckas
> and all manner of Blacks (negroes too) sweet
> muthafuckas, crazy muthafuckas, lowdown muthafuckas
> cool muthafuckas, mad and revolutionary muthafuckas.
> But anyhow you all know just like i do (whether i say
> it or not), there's plenty of MEAN muthafuckas out
> here trying to do the struggle in and we all know
> that none of us can relax until the last m.f.'s
> been done in.

So, too, Saloy writes:

> So, I hope that no card-carrying
> African American, or no stamped, certified,

Colored, or Negro is ever insulted
Cause I call a nigger **my nigger.**

Nigger please!

David Nelson, one of the so-called Original Last Poets, described the Last Poets' use of "nigger" as based on the belief, paraphrasing his own poem, "Die Nigger," that "the nigger needs to die so that black folks can take over" (Fernando, 133).

The intracommunity debate on language practice is part of a larger ongoing African American discussion about the role of the artist in a community that sees itself in struggle against forces that demean it and stereotype it. That African American poets continue to write about issues of language and representation is testament to the centrality of this dialogue. The blues, boast, and toast in African American vernacular culture have always occupied the realm of "the devil" or secular space. As such they have been the appropriate spaces in which to articulate outsider, outlaw, and rebel aspects of African American aspirations. The current bewailing of antisocial attitudes and nihilism in contemporary rap culture echoes criticism of the negative images of "Blaxploitation" films during the seventies and the use of profane language in the late sixties, which in turn echoed critics of the Harlem Renaissance, who disapproved of the focus on "lowlife" by writers of that period. The romanticizing of these elements both in the Black Arts and Black Revolution adherents as well as among antiestablishment white sociocultural forces was almost inevitable in the context of the United States in the late sixties and early seventies.

The kind of angst or nihilism present in the blues and identified as such in a poem such as Langston Hughes's "The Weary Blues," written in the late twenties, parallels the attitudes of Larry Neal's "Brother Pimp," of the late 1960s, which he dedicates to "Iceberg Slim" (the "hero" of a series of popular novels). While African American vernacular culture celebrates the outlaw for doing what the more law-abiding dare not do and relishes the defiant posture, the poet tries to convert the outlaw to more conscious struggle, much in the way that the Nation of Islam and the Black Panther Party attempted to recruit the lumpen into forces for righteous struggle. The pleasure that the audience or reader takes in the depiction of defiant characters and their anti-social words and deeds is an inducement to think about the pleasures of more significant words and deeds. The preacher's call to the mourners' bench, most explicitly in sermons on "The Prodigal Son" or "Sodom and Gomorrah," were and still are popular as much for their vivid depictions of sin as for their promises of salvation. To point out the persistence of a tradition or a long-standing cultural practice does not imply that such practices are "good," merely that they are not new. Exploring the range of literary practice engendered by vernacular practice enables an examination of change within tradition as well as outright disruptions of that tradition.

Another debated feature of the male-dominated discourse of boast and toast is its antiwoman language and attitude. Stephen Calt notes the misogyny of many blues lyrics, but Angela Davis (1998) has documented the protofeminism of the blues lyrics of Ma Rainey and Bessie Smith.[5] Bruce Jackson and Richard Abrahams point out the misogyny of most traditional toasts. Houston Baker, Nelson George, Tricia Rose, and Greg Tate all discuss at length the misogyny of contemporary hip-hop culture and rap lyrics. Yet just as African American women blues lyricists and poets voice contested issues between men and women in the folk vernacular and the literary spheres, contemporary female rappers voice an answer to that misogyny. Queen Latifah, in her boastful rap "Ladies First" and her challenge "U.N.I.T.Y." (see the discography), inserts her voice into the contemporary vernacular discussion:

> I break into a Liverpool freestyle,
> Grab the mike, look at the crowd and see smiles,
> Cause they see a woman stand up on her own two
> Sloppy, slouchin, insultin I won't do
> Some think that we can't flow
> Stereotypes, they got to go
> I will mess around and flip the scene into reverse
> (With what?) with a little touch of Ladies First.

Latifah claims both the right to the microphone and the ability to use it.

Similarly, toward the end of the Black Arts era, when the African American struggle was so often equated with a struggle for "Black Manhood," African American women poets not only challenged that equation but the very definitions of manhood itself. Jayne Cortez's 1977 poem, "If the Drum Is a Woman" (in *Coagulations*) issues a challenge:

But if the drum is a woman
why are you choking your drum
why are you raping your drum
why are you saying disrespectful things
to your mother drum your sister drum
your wife drum and your infant daughter drum
If the drum is a woman
then understand your drum
your drum is not docile
your drum is not invisible
your drum is not inferior to you
your drum is a woman

Concomitantly, these women poets entered the ongoing discussion about definitions of womanhood, part of African American literary discourse since the female slave narrative illuminated the contradictions between the definition of woman advanced by the dominant culture and the reality of the lives of slave women. June Jordan explores the many facets of African American womanhood in "Getting Down to Get Over" (in *Naming Our Destiny*):

MOMMA MOMMA MOMMA
momma momma
mammy
nanny
granny
woman
mistress
sista

luv

blackgirl
slavegirl

gal

honeychile
sweetstuff

sugar
sweetheart
baby
Baby Baby
MOMMA MOMMA
Black Momma
Black bitch
Black pussy
piecea tail
nice piecea ass

Jordan's three-part, toastlike poem, dedicated to her mother, explores African American female experience in terms of popular media stereotypes, history, and personal experience. It uses typical Black Arts metaphors, such as the African American woman as queen; and it revises that metaphor. Jordan's queen "works when she works." The poem adheres to convention in its call for an idealized male-female relationship—"teach me how to kiss/ the king within the kingdom"—but its conclusion—"help me/ turn the face of history/ *to your face*"—offers several messages. Whether we read the last line as "into" or "toward," the poem's call is for a centering of African American women's experience.

Like June Jordan's "Getting Down to Get Over" and Jayne Cortez's "If the Drum Is a Woman," Sonia Sanchez's haiku was published in the late seventies (in *I've Been a Woman*) as a new Black feminism was beginning to emerge.

who are you/ iden./
tify yourself. tell me your
worth amid women.

Such poems and others tell ghetto cautionary tales about muggings, rape and other forms of abuse. Earlier, the women poets of the New Black Arts movement, in addition to their poems of self-love, took as a primary mission the assertion of the worth of African American men. Although they did not hesitate to chastise men for their flaws, they also took it as their mission to give African American men "back their manhood."[6] However, these poets also called for female solidarity. The assertive voices of New

Black Arts women poets like Nikki Giovanni, Carolyn Rodgers, and Sonia Sanchez were joined by those of June Jordan and Audre Lorde, whose primary public identities were feminist.

Although the literary careers of Lorde and Jordan actually began during the New Black Arts movement, the ways in which literary periods get defined often have as much to do with which writers get singled out for attention as the actual quality and content of a writer's work. I have heard critic Gloria Hull revise African American literary history of the twenties so that its geographical center was Washington, D.C., and its central figures Georgia Douglas Johnson and Anne Spencer, with a "meanwhile in Harlem" conclusion.[7] If one examines African American poetry through the practice of its women poets, one finds many variations in subject and theme but stylistic practices shared with their poet brothers.

From Paul Laurence Dunbar to young poets such as Reg E. Gaines, Patricia Smith, Tracie Morris, and Saul Williams, African American poets have been oral readers and performers of their own work. African American poets have been recorded on records, tapes, audiocassettes, and compact discs. They continue to appear on radio and television and now take center stage in films and videos. Poets such as Langston Hughes in the twenties and thirties and Ntozake Shange in the seventies staged dramatic productions constructed from their poems. Theater companies and directors have mounted productions of African American poetry organized into a coherent drama or performance.[8] Across the United States, in innumerable church and school celebrations during Black History Month observances, some African American child, woman, or man rises to read a poem by an African American author. African American oral performance is so widespread that it is taken for granted.

Still another vernacular practice that informs the poets' work is the African American tall tale tradition. Sterling Brown and Langston Hughes were early practitioners of a literary rendition of the vernacular practice of "swapping lies." In these communal storytelling settings, the goal was to render the most outrageous tale. (The African American version of the American tall tale in its most widely known plot is the story of John Henry.)

> When Susanna Jones wears Red
> Her face is like an ancient cameo
> Turned brown by the ages
>
> . . . .

When Susanna Jones wears red
A queen from some time-dead Egyptian night
Walks once again.
Langston Hughes, "When Sue Wears Red"

When Annie Mae Johnson condescends to take the air,
Give up all your business, make haste to get there,
. . . .
The last time I saw Annie on the Avenue
She held up traffic for an hour or two
The green light refused, absolutely to go off at all;
And the red light and the amber nearly popped the glass,
When Annie walked by, they came on so fast.
Sterling Brown, "Glory, Glory"

The Hughes and Brown excerpts use hyperbole to humorous effect. Trumpets blow when Susanna wears red. Brown compares the effect of Annie Mae Johnson's walk to that of Moses parting the waters. (The juxtaposition of exclamations drawn from sacred culture with the purely secular social situations of the poems is another common vernacular practice.) Both Brown and Hughes were accomplished raconteurs in life. Brown's 1975 collection *The Last Ride of Wild Bill* consists almost entirely of poems in the tall tale tradition. They also were keen observers of the folk and their ways. They and subsequent generations of poets followed Dunbar's tradition of giving voice to the voiceless, documenting the lives and experiences of everyday people in a community.

In the nineties poets such as Reg E. Gaines in "Please Don't Take My Air Jordans" (in Algarin and Holman) and Jabari Asim in "Hip Hop Bop" (in Powell and Baraka) further extend these traditions of storytelling and celebration.

My air jordans cost a hundred with tax
my suede starters jacket says raiders on the back
I'm stylin . . . smilin . . . lookin real mean cuz
it ain't about bein heard just bein seen
Reg E. Gaines

I'm a hipster lindy-hoppin in the corner of mind
twirlin toward the exit, strivin ta find

the light of true poetic expression,
breakin the back of systematic oppression
liberatin language, demandin attention
helpin hip hop to another dimension
jazz & rap in combustible conflation
crazyfresh lyrical prestidigitation

Jabari Asim

When Reg E. Gaines gives voice to his gangsta, in his quest for respect through the acquisition of high-priced apparel, he is placing him and his brothers in front of an audience in a way that a rap video does not. By giving him voice and telling his story, Gaines claims significance for his life. Jabari Asim, on the other hand, assumes the rhythms, rhymes, and idioms of hip-hop culture through which to articulate his own mission as a poet. Gaines and Asim are heirs of Brown and Hughes, of Reed and Giovanni, and of the vernacular toast tradition, but they are also poets of the hip-hop generation and rap culture. Tricia Rose's 1994 study *Black Noise* analyzes rap music and culture noting how they prioritize "black voices from the margins of urban America" (2). African American hip-hop culture, including rap, is today a worldwide phenomenon influenced by and influencing Caribbean and British Dub, generating a francophone Parisian-African style of rap as well as an anglophone South African one. A similar cross-fertilization is taking place as African American poets and their works travel across the "Black Atlantic" from the United States to Africa, the Caribbean, and Europe.

African American poetry extends vernacular culture by providing a means of continuity and permanence. African American poets share with both the blues lyricist and the rapper the task of giving voice to the silent and silenced. Since rap lyrics are both written and recorded, African American poetry at the end of the twentieth century can be seen as mediating between a folk orality and a technologized orality. As oral folk culture gave way to a popular electronic one, print carried stories and characters and forms into the age of electronic media. Popular culture, in turn, offers new vocabulary, characters, and forms as poetic inspiration. In poetry the richest strains of vernacular expression are revised and retained and re-created in the next generation.

In African American culture, poetry provides popular entertainment. Writers' workshops can be found not only on college campuses but also in local African American bookstores, in neighborhood libraries, in church halls, and in community living rooms. When a group of African American workers decide to hold a Black History Month observance at their workplace, they often invite a poet or an actor to come read poetry. When an African American women's club or sorority celebrate themselves or their heritage, poetry is on the program. In the community college composition classroom, inevitably a student will bring in some poems for the teacher to read. African American rappers pay homage to the poets, and the younger and not-so-young poets pay tribute to the rappers. Maya Angelou records with Ashford and Simpson. Nikki Giovanni and Sonia Sanchez dedicate their 1997 collections of love poems to deceased rapper Tupac Shakur. Sonia Sanchez appears on the late-night television program *Vibe* to pay poetic tribute to rapper Rakim. And rapper/poet Derrick Gilbert, AKA D-Knowledge, compiles a multigenerational anthology of African American poetry. The tradition continues.

"Black Is ... and Black Ain't"

*Of Gender and Generations in
African American Poetry*

CHAPTER 6

There's more to being black than meets the eye.
CHARLES GORDONE

"It's a Black Thing . . ."
T-SHIRT SLOGAN

In previous chapters, I have argued that an examination of African American vernacular culture, particularly in its expressive and performance aspects, informs our understanding of African American poetry. Among the ramifications of such an approach, two related questions seem especially worth exploring. What is the place of gender or sexuality in vernacular practice? How does vernacular tradition manifest itself, if at all, in the current generation of poets, male or female, heterosexual or homosexual?

Men and women share a vernacular culture, yet they experience culture, a way of life after all, with a gendered difference. The differences are not between the public and the private, as is often asserted—men are capable of introspection, of meditations on family life and relationships, and women write public and political verse—but in the choice of subjects and themes.

But how do women participate in or extend African American vernacular? In a 1977 conversation, the poet/scholar Gloria Hull raised the question of whether it might be possible to identify an African American woman's way of using language. Every time I think I can answer the question affirmatively, I find an example of a male poet using language in a similar fashion. Erlene Stetson, in the introduction to her 1980 anthology, *Black Sister,* identifies a "black feminist poetic tradition" in which "music, particularly the blues, has provided themes, images, structures, and poetic devices" (xiv–xv). As was shown in my chapter on song/talk, music, including the blues, is an essential element in African American poetry, written by men or women. The importance of musical elements is not a sufficient answer to Hull's questions.

Male and female blues artists share a body of verses in the oral recorded tradition. The late Junior Wells recorded Tracy Chapman's blues song "Give Me One Reason," and made it his own. In the rhythm and blues tradition, Aretha Franklin took Otis Redding's "Respect" and turned into an anthem of both a racial and a female assertion of entitlement. Similarly, male and female poets work the continuum of vernacular blues culture. "When a woman gets the blues," sings the old song, "she goes in her room and hides. When a man gets the blues, he grabs a train and rides." However, both men and women sing this song. "If I had wings," sang the washerwoman Dink in the song that bears her name, "like Norah's dove, I'd fly away to the man I love." Men have recorded this song too.[1] The metaphor of flight is buried deep in the vernacular. It can be found variously in the stories and songs about the flying Africans, in the spirituals such as "Let Me Fly," and in popular culture in a song like "I Believe I Can Fly," written by R. Kelly as an anthem for a Michael Jordan movie. That African American vernacular metaphor combines in the literature with the Greek myth of Daedalus and Icarus and the universal human longing for flight.[2] When a woman dreams and sings of flight as a metaphor for escape, how is that different from the dreams and songs of a man? Perhaps the difference in the use of the metaphor lies in what the woman desires to escape from or fly to.

African American vernacular tradition is one shared by the sexes. In some cases, the space in which they perform is the same—such as the fields or the blues club or jook joint. There are also gendered spaces such as the beauty shop and barber shop or male work gang and men or women's prison. Still other spaces offer different roles to the sexes along the order of "men preach and women pray." But men do pray and women do preach.

Paul Gilroy, in a discussion of Black music, asserts that "gender is the modality in which race is lived" (85). Reading gender into an exploration of a racial vernacular would then lead us into an exploration of the modalities of gender within that vernacular. Erlene Stetson explores such modalities and fleshes out her claim that African American women poets have created symbols "that are uniquely black and female" (xv). Their tradition is not one based on style but one that "shows wide variations in form and technique. Their themes and subjects have developed over the generations out of common historical experience." She goes on to posit an "underlying unity of theme, strategy, and symbol" (xvii). It is in the symbolic universe that Stetson looks for a particularly female modality of utterance. She goes on to articulate three constructs in her discussion of African American women poets: "a compelling quest for identity, a subversive perception of reality, and subterfuge and ambivalence as creative strategies" (xvii). Although we might find evidence of these constructs in poems by African American men, there is sufficient evidence to include them in our definition of a female difference. I have already discussed the ways in which indirection is a nongendered vernacular practice. Similarly, the quest for identity is a racial one that is expressed in gendered terms as in the old slave plaints: "Am I not a man and a brother? Am I not a woman and a sister?" "Who am I, black in a white world" is a shared theme while "Who am I, black woman," or "Who am I, black man," is another. And "Who am I" is still another. Each question connotes another kind of specificity.

African American women poets are not only participants in a tradition. They are unacknowledged makers of the tradition. African American written poetic tradition begins with two women: Lucy Terry, whose 1746 poem, "Bars' Fight," is acknowledged as the first poem published by an African American; and Phillis Wheatley, whose 1771 *Poems on Various Subjects* is the first volume of poems published by an African American. We find traces of a female voice, too, in the domestic images of spirituals about "the welcoming table" and about Mary and Martha. And surely it was a woman's voice that sang about "poor little Jesus." From the "black and unknown [female] bards" who created spirituals to the unknown folk blues lyricists, to the storytellers around the kitchen tables, to the "sisters" standing in front of the churches on Sunday mornings, to the hairdressers standing over shampoo bowls and hot combs, African American women have made and continue to make their voices heard in women's spaces within vernacular culture. The womanly changes on African American vernacular traditions also manifest themselves in the jump-rope, particularly double Dutch, rhymes made by girls in a manner similar to the swaggering braggadocio found in the street rhymes of boys. Both are signifying traditions carried forward into today's hip-hop lyrics on rap recordings by both female and male artists. When Queen Latifah claims a microphone, she claims space in the manner of Maria

Stewart in eighteenth-century pulpits, of Frances Harper on the abolitionist lecture circuit, of the unknown women who offered up prayer on behalf of congregations every week, and of all the girls and women called upon to recite a poem for the church or school program.

In fact, as Tricia Rose points out, young African American women have claimed their own space in rap and hip-hop culture. "Young African-American women provide for themselves a relatively safe free-play zone where they creatively address questions of sexual power, the reality of truncated economic opportunity, and the pain of racism and sexism" (146). In the sacred and in the secular vernacular tradition, female voices have claimed a space. The cry is not merely one that claims humanity, but one that claims womanhood in Black. "I am a Black woman," writes Mari Evans.

Looking then to the symbolic universe of poetry by African American women, we find that these artists claim their own angle of vision on the world. They not only claim voice and a platform, but they write and speak with authority, one claimed by right of heritage as well as selfhood. Erlene Stetson writes:

> Since the eighteenth century, black women have explored a personal landscape in their poetry through symbols of flowers and houses. The house represents the historic quest by black women for homes of their own—apart from the house of slavery, the common house of bondage, the house of the patriarch. The house embodies women's search for place and belonging and for a whole and complete identity, as well as representing the historical house that was so difficult to get. In addition, the house is a symbol for place—heaven, haven, home, the heart, women's estate, the earthly tenement, the hearth—and for region—Africa, the West Indies, American, Asia, the North, and the South (xxii).

Stetson's analysis of the symbolism of the house is so broad and all-inclusive as to render that symbol almost meaningless. Her symbolic flower is equally broad. "The flower is an image of rootedness and, by contrast, rootlessness. Flowers symbolize the cultural diversity of women; like flowers, black women are rooted in the culture of which they are a part" (xxiii). The contrast between metaphorical flowers rooted in the earth and those uprooted for display or for disposal opens an arena she does not explore.

Maureen Honey, in her anthology of women poets of the Harlem

Renaissance, posits a "symbolic landscape of nature and romantic love" in which "to affirm the humanitiy of women rendered invisible by the dominant culture" (3). Honey argues that "as Afro-Americans, women poets were sensitive to the political and artistic currents affecting Black men of their day, but as women, they drew special meaning from them" (7). Women poets of the Harlem Renaissance, according to Honey, "saw the cityscape as [literally] manmade" and the "urban environment as alien and intrusive. Nature, in contrast, is presented as nurturing, life-giving, a haven from strife [and] often also personified as female" (8). Although Honey concedes that the women poets might share a pastoral vision with such male poets as Countee Cullen and Claude McKay, she asserts that "nature provided an objective correlative . . . for gender oppression. . . . Nature, like them, had been objectified, invaded, and used by men seeking power and wealth" (8). Honey and Stetson begin the task of a feminist critique of poetry by African American women. I believe that task remains uncompleted.

In the language of African American women poets we might find a kind of double veiling, the encoding of both race and gender. When June Jordan writes, "I must become a menace to my enemies" (*Things That I Do in the Dark*), one can read the poem from the perspective of race or gender or both. African American women poets demand that we read their works as statements of African American women. Gender and race are inseparable, parts of one integral whole.

> I will no longer lightly walk behind
> a one of you who fear me:
> > Be afraid
> I plan to give you reason for your jumpy fits
> and facial tics
> I will not walk politely on the pavements anymore
> and this is dedicated in particular
> to those who hear my footsteps
> or the insubstantial rattling of my grocery
> cart
> then turn around
> see me
> and hurry on
> away from this terror I must be:

Jordan's poem, dedicated to the first president of Angola, the poet Agostinho Neto, contains layers of meaning. The 1976 poem was written within the context of the liberation struggles of southern Africa and struggles against police brutality within the urban United States. But the poem was also written during the second wave of American feminism. The speaking voice of the poem is both African American and woman. Who is the "you" that the poem addresses, then? The answer to that question determines our reading of the poem.

Jordan, an African American woman, can speak to apartheid South Africa's power at the same time as she addresses a white power structure in the United States and a male patriarchy, white or black. The "you" is all of the above.

> I plan to blossom bloody on an afternooon
> surrounded by my comrades singing
> terrible revenge in merciless
> accelerating
> rhythms

Stetson's flowers resonate in these lines juxtaposed with images of final judgment. But rather than homey images of gardens and rootedness, Jordan's blossoms emerge bloody, birthed into revolution. (Note also the rhythmic effect of the varying line lengths.) Jordan claims the cityscape (in which to find her bloody garden?) as well.

> I live like a lover
> who drops her dime into the phone
> just then the subway shakes into the station
> wasting her message
> cancelling the question of her call:

Jordan's jeremiad fits into an African American vernacular tradition that recognizes, though often grudgingly, a woman's right to preach. In African American vernacular tradition, it is not only the "right to sing the blues" that belongs to the woman. She also has the right to preach and lead. Although the traditionally assigned role of the woman is that of prayer, African American women long ago claimed the pulpit as well.[3] The explicit use of the female pronouns and the domestic allusions to a shopping cart and setting a table identify a female speaker, albeit a very militant one.

The only overt racial elements in the poem are references to Angola in the poem's dedication, to South Africa in the body of the poem, and to "my brothers and my sisters" in the first line of the second part of the poem.

> How many of my brothers and my sisters
> will they kill
> before I teach myself
> retaliation?
> shall we pick a number?
> South Africa for instance:
> do we agree that more than ten thousand
> in less than a year but less than
> five thousand slaughtered in more than six
> months will
> WHAT IS THE MATTER WITH ME?

Perhaps we might read "(the blossoming flamingoes of my/ wild mimosa trees)" toward the end of the poem as a racial clue to an African or Caribbean landscape. However, the lines even more strongly suggest sensuality and female identity connected to the earlier "blossom bloody." They identify a call to arms by a woman warrior. It is probably our knowledge as readers that the poet is an African American woman that enables us to read the poem racially. Its female vocalization is overt.

On the other hand, Mari Evans, who came to prominence as a poet during the New Black Arts movement,[4] issues a quieter, more indirect, call to arms. Her poem, "Whisper Together Brethren," signals its speaker's race, not gender.

> Whisper together brethren
> Glide thru the darkness
> Thru the darkness black
> like you
> Thru ancestral blackness
> Glide alone, in pairs
> Thru ancestral blackness where one match

> Burns brighter than a thousand slogans and one
>   bullet speaks
> Louder than a million marching feet
> For every Black Man's murdered back
> Death is the equalizer
> There is a company among us
> That should have ceased to be . . .
> Whisper together brethren
> Glide through the darkness

Just as our knowledge of Jordan's race enables a racial reading of her poem, I believe our knowledge of Evans's gender enables a gendered reading of her poem. Maureen Honey's reading of "veiled references to race and gender oppression in women's poetry of the Harlem Renaissance" (10) might apply to women's poetry of the New Black Arts movement as well. During an era when "Black Power" was so often written as male, female assertions of authority and power often were veiled. The incantatory rhythms and hushed tones of Evans's poem suggest a female priestly voice, even as the speaker revises the oratory of Malcolm X. In an era when raised male voices were the norm, the cautionary "whisper together" sounds female, evoking the hushed tones of General Harriet Tubman leading slaves to freedom.

African American women poets often enter the discourse as daughters, sisters, mothers, and lovers, that is, in relationship to others, both male and female. Those relationships often become the subjects of their poems. Even more often, though, those relationships constitute the stance from which the women write. Thus, Mari Evans's exhortations to her brethren to "whisper together" can be read as both sisterly and priestly caution. Lucille Clifton's "Harriet" provides another way of reading gender in poems by African American women:

> if i be you
> let me not forget
> to be the pistol
> pointed
> to be the madwoman
> at the rivers edge

warning
be free or die
and isabel
if I be you
let me in my
sojourning
not forget
to ask my brothers
ain't I a woman too
and
grandmother
if I be you
let me not forget to
work hard
trust the Gods
love my children and
wait.

Clifton's poem asserts a matrilineal lineage that includes Harriet Tubman and Sojourner Truth as well as her own grandmother. In other poems, she directly addresses her daughters rather than the more inclusive "children." Writing as an intermediary between previous and future generations, the poet is not only mother but also daughter—an heir to a tradition. *Work, trust, love,* and *wait* are the imperatives urged in this prayer.

Women writers seem to have a more personal investment in future generations than do male writers. From her *Bronzeville Boys and Girls* to her *Children Coming Home,* Gwendolyn Brooks writes children's poems for adults. Adopting the stance of wise woman and mother, she gives voice to children who pass on adult wisdom, like Kojo in *Children Coming Home,* for example, who states:

I Am a Black

According to my teachers,
I am now an African-American.

They call me out of my name.

BLACK is an open umbrella.
I am Black and A Black forever.

I am one of The Blacks.

We are Here, we are There,
We occur in Brazil, in Nigeria, Ghana,
in Botswana, Tanzania, in Kenya,
in Russia, Australia, in Haiti, Soweto,
in Grenada, in Cuba, in Panama, Libya
in England and Italy, France.

We are graces in any places
I am Black and A Black
forever.

I say, proudly, MY PEOPLE!
I say, proudly, OUR PEOPLE!

Our people do not disdain to eat yams or melons or grits
or put peanut butter in stew.

I am Kojo. In West Afrika Kojo
means Unconquerable. My parents
named me the seventh day from my birth
in Black spirit, Black Faith, Black communion.
I am Kojo. I am A Black.
And I Capitalize my name.

Do not call me out of my name.

Brooks's voicings, not only of children, but of adults as well, articulate
the multiple variations of personality and opinion to be found among
African Americans. Like Clifton, Brooks loves her children for who
they are and who they can be. Praise poems for children and grandpar-
ents, especially grandmothers, also express introspection. African American women poets measure themselves against the accomplishments of their
foremothers and sometimes don't measure up. They also worry about the

nature of the world they are leaving to their children. This expression of a personal stake in the future marks apocalyptic preachments such as Johari Amini's "untitled" and June Jordan's "I Must Become a Menace to My Enemies."

Poems of familial, romantic, and erotic love abound in the works of African American women. Angelina Weld Grimke, Georgia Douglas Johnson, and Anne Spencer wrote poems of longing and desire that serve as foremothers to lyrics of their literary daughters from Gwendolyn Brooks to Angela Jackson to Tracie Morris. The language becomes more explicit over the decades as women's voices become more assertive. From Johnson's "I want to die while you love me" to Jackson's "I'm gon put a hex on you/ work some voo-doo magic/ on/ yo mind," women poets express their ardor in the literary and social conventions of their day. Thus, the passivity indicated in Johnson's language gives way to the aggressive stance of Jackson's. Today women can be overt wooers as well as the wooed. They also can express themselves in sexual as well as sensual language. Overt expressions of sexuality and desire are markers of expanding feminist consciousness.

African American women poets such as Frances Harper in the late nineteenth century and Anne Spencer in the early twentieth century articulated "feminist" ideas in their poems. That both of these women found in the biblical character of Vashti (from the Book of Esther) a means of exploring oppressive conditions of women, Harper in 1895 and Spencer in 1920, is probably coincidental. That they and other women poets write about women and give voice to women real and imagined is not. African American women poets assume a public space and the right to speak out of a heritage of equal employment during slavery and double jeopardy in freedom. Their praise poems to their foremothers and sisters in struggle celebrate that legacy even as they lament its costs. Equality with men is a birthright and is assumed. Women poets note and document the importance of women's lives and experiences. Giving voice to women and telling women's stories, women poets extend the vernacular tradition of women claiming their own space and making their voices heard.

Discussions of maleness and femaleness are complicated by considerations of sexuality. Just as a period of female assertiveness brought us to a consideration of gendered discourse, today we must also become conscious of the ways in which sexuality affects discourse. Audre Lorde always described herself as "Black, lesbian, mother, warrior, woman poet."

Her self-naming is itself a poem in the vernacular tradition—a naming of qualities, attributes, selves that constitute her complete identity. Lorde's earliest volume of poetry was published by Broadside Press, a publisher viewed as nationalist, read male-centered. Yet her poetry, even during this period, was sometimes overtly lesbian. She insisted on a definition of "Blackness" that included her. In very many ways, Audre Lorde made it possible for other lesbian poets like Pat Parker and Kate Rushin to enter the public sphere. Her "Litany for Survival" issues a challenge to African American gay and lesbian poets:[5]

> and when we speak we are afraid
> our words will not be heard
> nor welcomed
> but when we are silent
> we are still afraid.
> So it is better to speak
> remembering
> we were never meant to survive.

Again it is our knowledge of the identity of the writer that enables our reading. Indeed, the poem has something to say to anyone among the oppressed and voiceless. Our knowledge that the poet is a woman enables us to read the poem in the context of feminist struggle while our knowledge that Lorde is both African American and lesbian enables still more specific readings of these lines.

> Woman Power
> is
> Black Power
> Is
> Human Power

These lines begin the poem "Now," originally published by Broadside Press in *The New York Head Shop and Museum* (and later in *Chosen Poems—Old and New*). Omitted from this 1973 poem is the phrase "Gay and Lesbian Power." However, other poems in this collection do reveal Lorde's lesbian identity. What this poem makes clear is the need for expanded definitions of both Blackness and humanity.

The anthology of African American gay and lesbian poetry has yet to be compiled. I am aware of two collections of African American gay writing, *In the Life,* edited by Joseph Beam in 1986, and *Brother to Brother,* edited by Essex Hemphill in 1991, and one collection of African American lesbian writing, *Afrikete,*[6] edited by Catherine E. McKinley and L. Joyce Delaney in 1995. The two gay anthologies include forty-three poems, including eight by Hemphill. Part II of his elegiac poem, "The Tomb of Sorrow" (in *Brother to Brother*), includes this stanza:

> When I die,
> honey chil',
> my angels
> will be tall
> Black drag queens
> I will eat their stockings
> as they fling them
> into the blue
> shadows of dawn
> I will suck
> their purple lips
> to anoint my mouth
> for the utterance of prayers

Some of the imagery in the poem calls to mind a poem by Patricia Spears Jones, "The Perfect Lipstick":

> It is why I appreciate my favorite shade of lipstick:
> Sherry Velour.
>
> Sounds like the name of a drag queen from the early seventies.
> One of those strapping Black men who had enough of playing
>   macho,
> put their feet in five-inch heels and made saints of Dinah
>   Washington
> Rita Hayworth and a very young Nina Simone.
>
> So, on goes this lipstick. Pretty for parties.
> Fatal for festivals.

Sherry Velour and her hot discoveries:
. . . .
Black men in sequinned dresses and the click of new words
in the new world where the most dangerous of dreams
come true.

Hemphill's poem blends elements of the sacred and the profane, echoing the cry of the spiritual, "I want to die easy when I die," and revising
the blues cry for "six white horses and plenty pretty women" into "tall
Black drag queens" and "immaculate Black divas." Jones's poem points
to an overlooked aspect of African American vernacular culture: as an "outsider" culture, African American vernacular also has its own outsiders.
Homosexuals, particularly the "butch" lesbian and the drag queen or effem-
inate gay male, become metaphors for both the extraordinary and the ter-
rible. The close relationship between African American gay men and
African American women, both straight and gay, is visible and audible
in their language. "Girl Friend," the ultimate epithet of closeness among
African American women, is appropriated by gay men as auditory punctuation that signals their "difference."

When Melvin Dixon tells the story of how "Aunt Ida pieces a quilt"
(in Hemphill, *Brother to Brother*), he gives Aunt Ida voice and places the
AIDS quilt in the African American vernacular art of quilting:

They brought me some of his clothes. The hospital gown
those too-tight dungarees, his blue choir robe
with the gold sash. How that boy could sing!
His favorite color in a necktie. A Sunday shirt.
What I'm gonna do with all this stuff?
I can remember Junie without this business.
My niece Francine say they quilting all over the country.
So many good boys like her boy gone.

The colloquial voice of the opening stanza takes us through Aunt Ida's
remembrances of the dead young man. Her digressions fill out a portrait
of a family and a community, and ultimately a nation, that has suffered
a great loss. Dixon stitches together elements of Aunt Ida and Junie, the
"boy," creating a portrait of the two as patches in the quilt of a family.

Vernacular elements of family amd church choirs and a community's ambivalence toward flamboyant homosexual men are woven into the larger tapestry of the AIDS epidemic as represented in the AIDS quilt. Aunt Ida stitches her name in red on the back of every quilt she makes. "That's where Junie got his flair" says the poet. Aunt Ida's niece, Francene, wants to hang the quilt in church where her son Junie sang. Then she wants to send it to Washington as part of the NAMES quilt display. The poem is both elegy and preachment. "Maybe we all like that, patches waiting to be pieced": one quilt—one family, one community, one nation. Too many of the poems of *In the Life* and *Brother to Brother* are elegies, echoes of the prison lament, "Another Man Done Gone," and reverberations of other elegies, for young men killed in urban strife. African American gay poets enter the vernacular discourse in the deep purple of mourning.[7]

In the introduction to *Brother to Brother,* Essex Hemphill writes, "We must begin to identify what a black gay sensibility is; identify its esthetic, qualities and components; identify specific constructions and uses of language suitable for the task of presenting our experiences in the context of literature, and then determine how this sensibility and esthetic relates to and differs from African American literature as a whole" (xxvii). Like Gloria Hull, in her explorations of women's voicings, Hemphill wants to identify a difference within a racial difference. In the same volume Charles I. Nero, in an essay entitled "Toward a black gay aesthetic," attempts to define that difference. "First, the use of signifiying by black gay men places their writing squarely within the African American literary tradition. Second, signifying permits black gay men to revise the 'Black Experience' in African American literature and, thereby, to create a space for themselves."

It is important to note that Nero identifies the African American vernacular practice and literary trope of signifying as the site of African American gay male difference. African American gay men signify on conventional notions of gender and gender difference, often assuming a kind of literary drag. Nero goes on to explore the ways in which African American gay poets signify on "representations of desire, the black religious experience, and gender configurations" (231). He singles out the ways in which the poetry of the late Essex Hemphill revises African American culture's ideas about masculinity and male sexual desire and love. Similarly, African American lesbian poets revise traditional notions of womanhood and female sexual desire and love as they signify on vernacular practices of female community. Kate Rushin announces a lesbian lineage when she writes of her "Family Tree" (in *The Black Back Ups*):

> I come from
> A long line of
> Uppity Irate Black Women

Writing out of a woman-centered vernacular culture, Rushin claims a space for her own lesbian identity within that culture. She writes of the contestations for that space in "The Invisible Woman":

> I am The Invisible Woman
> Super Woman
> Wonder Woman
> Afro Woman
> The Woman with Triple Vision
> . . . .
> I listen to my relatives talk about
> Homos, fags, fairies
> And that girl who walks like a man
> Something tells me
> I was not supposed to hear this
> Something tells me
> I was not supposed to see this
> Something tells me
> I was not supposed to be here
> Something tells me
> You do not see me

Rushin selects as an epigraph for her poem a quotation from Ralph Ellison's prologue to his novel *Invisible Man* about the advantages of invisibilty, "although it is most often rather wearing on the nerves." Like Ellison's racially invisible man, Rushin's invisible lesbian woman becomes visible through an act of language. She indirectly chastises the careless homophobic speech in her family and community and claims her space.

Just as African American women challenge sexism within the culture and without, African American gay men and lesbians challenge

homophobia, both within the culture and without. They challenge nar-
row definitions of blackness, manhood, and womanhood. They also
argue for an indivisibility of oppression. Their "triple vision" imbues them
with authority to speak. Audre Lorde's poem "Who Said It Was Simple"
points to the complexity of the ways in which multiple identities challenge integrated existence.

> There are so many roots to the tree of anger
> that sometimes the branches shatter
> before they bear.
>
> Sitting in Nedicks
> the women rally before they march
> discussing the problematic girls
> they hire to make them free
> An almost white counterman passes
> a waiting brother to serve them first
> and the ladies neither notice nor reject
> the slightest pleasures of their slavery
> But I who am bound by my mirror
> as well as my bed
> see causes in colour
> as well as sex.
>
> and sit here wondering
> which me will survive
> all these liberations.

Lorde's ironic speaker notes the contradictions in the behavior of the people
under her gaze: the "women" marching for women's liberation unaware
of the race and class biases apparent in their discussion of their maids,
housekeepers, and nannies, who are "the problematic girls," and their accep-
tance of the privilege granted them because of the internalized racism of
the "almost white counterman." "Bound by my mirror/ as well as my bed,"
the speaker sees "causes in colour/ as well as sex": the words provide clues
to the speaker of the poem—her race, sexuality, and gender. The poet's
lesbian identity—contained in the reference to her bed—requires that "all
these liberations" include that sexuality as well as race and gender.

African American gay and lesbian poets and women poets claim a vernacular that includes them. They present themselves "in the tradition." And readers take for granted that they are African American poets.[8]

Although I have been arguing for African American vernacular and its cultural traditions, writing and making poetry remains a highly idiosyncratic art. Each poet makes the tradition new. Her or his voice works the changes on African American vernacular speech, or language practice, and its performance traditions. Each poet delights us with something new, as can be seen in the work of the contemporary generation of African American poets.

It is perhaps the rush to the new, so characteristic of the culture of the United States, that accounts for the academic interest in rap poetry. Aldon Nielsen, in his study of African American poetry, *Black Chant,* takes the critical establishment to task for overpraising rap artists as poets while ignoring both the jazz artists who write/ recite poetry as well as the jazz tradition in African American poetry. Nielsen's observations ring true. We need only look to contemporary media culture and its commodification of cultural expression to see some of the reasons. I have discussed some of the ways in which such artists as Gil Scott-Heron and the Last Poets as well as the poets of the New Black Arts movement are present in the language and performance styles of contemporary rap artists. Nielsen argues that "the formal differences among the African American poets [of different generations] can be read now as almost a call and response . . . a continuity between metrical formalism and the radical formalism of projective verse and the Black Arts [movement] as well as contemporary rhythmic experiments" (45). Nielsen again is calling our attention to the hybridity of African American poetry. His observations point to the ways in which African American poets appropriate and revise literary and vernacular practices. Today's younger African American poets, for whom rap is a presence in the vernacular, sometimes revise in rap the work of Langston Hughes, Sonia Sanchez, Amiri Baraka, and Nikki Giovanni, as well as of Gil Scott-Heron and others.

Tricia Rose, in her study of rap music, *Black Noise,* explores practices that might be useful to our understanding of current trends in African American poetry. "Rap lyrics are a critical part of a rapper's identity, strongly suggesting the importance of authorship and individuality in rap music. Yet sampling as it is used by rap artists indicates the importance of collective identities and group histories. There are hundreds of shared phrases and slang words in rap lyrics, yet a given rap text is the personal and emotive voice of the rapper. . . . Rap lyrics. . . articulate a distinct oral past" (95). Rose's observations illuminate the ways in which individual artists participate in and extend a tradition. The "changing same" of African American vernacular practice is observable in the interaction between folk and popular culture with literary practice.

Today, recordings preserve not only musical traditions but also poetic ones. Poetry is available in print, on recordings, and live in performance. Not only African American music in all its variations, from spirituals, blues, and gospel to rhythm and blues, jazz, and rap, but Black World music also is available. The sounds of Caribbean patois and West African pidgin have made their way to the United States through music as much as through immigration. Houston Baker, in *Black Studies, Rap and the Academy,* points out that young African Americans often approach poetry through the prism of rap. They "believe the function of poetry belongs in our era to a telecommunal, popular space in which a global audience interacts with performative artists. A link between music and performance—specifically popular music and performance—seems determative in their definition of the current and future function of poetry" (94). For Baker, poetry, like rap, "can be defined . . . as an audible sounding space of opposition" (95). The concept of the functionality of the language arts of song and story is embedded in African American vernacular culture. Indeed, my observation of other cultures of the African world lead me to believe that this concept is widespread in African and African diaspora cultures.

If, to quote Litte Richard, "the blues had a baby, and they named it rock and roll," which had to be reclaimed by a Black Rock Coalition and revised by others into rap, perhaps we might also say that the Harlem Renaissance had a baby, and they named it the New Black Arts movement, which has been revised as African American postmodernism. A 1998 anthology of poetry, *Catch the Fire!!!,* has as its subtitle, "A Cross-Generational Anthology of Contemporary African American Poetry." The anthology, as part of its strategy of assertion, includes prefatory section interviews by the editor, Derrick I. M. Gilbert (a.k.a. D-Knowledge), with the poets Amiri Baraka, June Jordan, Sonia Sanchez, Ntozake Shange, Quincy Troupe, and Abioodun Oyewole of the Last Poets. By name and by structure, the anthology announces the continuation of a tradition. Paul Gilroy's discussion of tradition in *The Black Atlantic* identifies a key factor in the maintenance of cultural traditions: "The idea of tradition gets understandably invoked to underscore the historical continuities, subcultural conversations, intertextual and intercultural cross-fertilisations which make the notion of a distinctive and self-conscious black culture appear plausible" (188). Artists self-consciously place themselves within a tradition whether by acknowledging the influence of foremothers and forefathers or by pointing out the ways in which they are breaking free of the strictures of a tradition.

Saul Williams, a Poetry Slam champion, writes his performance in "Recitation" (in Gilbert):

> i could recite the grass on a hill
>   and memorize the moon
>
>   i know the cloud forms of love by heart
> and love brought tears to the eye of the storm
>
> my memory banks vault of autumn forests
>   and amazon riverbanks
>
>   and i've screamed them into sunsets
> that echoed in earthquakes
>
> shadows have been my spotlights
>   as I monologue the night
>   and dialogue with days
> soliloquies of wind and breeze
>   applauded by sun rays
>   ***
>   we put language in zoo
>   to observe caged thought
> and tossed peanuts and p-funk at intellect
>
> and muthafuckas think these are metaphors
>   i speak what I see
> all words and worlds are metaphors of me
>
> my life is authored by the moon
>   footprints written in soil

> (I am)
> the fountain pen of martian men
>   novelling human soil
> and, yes, the soil speaks highly of me
>   when earth-seeds root me
>   poet-tree
>
>
> and we forest forever with recitation

Williams's poem exists in a tradition of language and metaphor to which he self-consciously calls our attention within the poem. His use of nature imagery revises Anglo-American pastoralism with an African American flair of blues-tinged surrealism. The occasional rhymes and allusion to "p-funk" call our attention to the song/talk of the poem and remind us that its author is a slam poet who recites his work aloud. His "poet-tree" revises the banalities of Joyce Kilmer's "Trees." Williams rejects the placement of language "in zoos" and "caged thought." He claims a public space, a landscape for his poetry. His shift from the lower case "i" within and at the end of the poem places the poet within a community at the same time that he claims outsider status, "the fountain pen of martian men." This "poet-tree" is rooted in a "forest of recitations."

Kevin Powell's "Out of Pocket" (in Gilbert) mixes allusions to hound dogs and minstrel shows with current events and titles of songs and books from high and low African American culture:

> I wanna be where you are sam
> right there on the stand with my man
>   oh-jay
> cock-blocking the souls of black folks
> sniffing glue with the spook who knocked down the door

Powell uses hip-hop rhythms to comment on the culture wars within African American culture on the contents of rap lyrics even as he himself castigates rappers for their narrowness of vision. The poem complicates questions of language, class and culture with its mix of allusions, colloquialisms, and profanity. Powell draws on hip-hop attitudes and language while he critiques its politics. Similar in attitude and style to Mari Evans's earlier "revolutionary" poem, "Vive Noir," his poem achieves the fervor of righteous preachment. Powell honors his ancestors and his peers as he riffs on the uses and misuses of language.

Each generation brings its own vocabulary and its own set of issues to the mix that constitutes African American vernacular culture, including its poetry. Gender, including sexuality, and generations mark the changes on the tradition of the vernacular "same." Saying this to say that, making words tap dance, swing, and sing, African American poets assert individual identities as they affirm community. They chronicle the history and tell the stories. They call down judgments and preach a new day. The self-defined and defining tradition that constitutes African American literary practice, particularly poetry, is a significant part of the whole that constitutes African American expressive culture. African American poets extend vernacular expression into the literary. Their poetic language exists within a continuum of language practice embedded in the performative and expressive practices that constitute African American vernacular culture. Their poetry is simply a "scriptive" way of performing the word.

Notes

INTRODUCTION

1. I use the terms "African" to refer to those who originate on the African continent and "African diaspora" to refer to those of African descent outside of Africa. I use the term "Black" as inclusive of both African and African diaspora and "African American" in reference to that part of the African diaspora which originates in the United States. Following such usages as Irish American, I do not hyphenate African American.

2. Historically, African American writers have been criticized as "mocking birds" in the nineteenth century and as provincials for "writing about Negroes too much" in the twentieth.

3. Of course, today, Langston Hughes, Robert Hayden, Gwendolyn Brooks, and Rita Dove show up in American literary anthologies with regularity, usually represented by the same few poems. But only rarely are examples from their work used to illustrate a lesson.

4. Writing as LeRoi Jones in *Black Music* (1967).

5. Gwendolyn Brooks uses the word "preachment" to describe and subtitle several of her poems. The first use appears around 1990.

6. "Nuyorican" is a term applied to Puerto Ricans living in New York; "Spanglish" is a blend of English and Spanish vocabulary and syntax.

CHAPTER I: MOTHER TONGUE

1. Pidgin is the term applied to a first step in language acquisition and development. It includes a basic vocabulary of a language with terms from the first language of its speakers and a stripped-down syntax sufficient for communication. "Creole" represents a more advanced stage of language acquisition in which the language retains aspects of the first and second languages, but is clearly a version or dialect of the second. Thus, West African pidgin in all its variations and Caribbean patois represent pidgin versions of English, while Caribbean English and African American vernacular English are types of creoles.

2. A "language act" is a type of utterance, such as a sermon. A language event is the context in which the act occurs, the service in which the sermon is preached; and a language situation includes the totality of act and event, that is, the preaching of the sermon with its congregational responses.

3. *Orature* is a term used among Africanists to describe what some call "oral literature," that is, the sayings, songs, and so on that comprise the matter of oral tradition. Isidore Okpewho is among those who have written extensively on African orature.

4. The *Oxford American Dictionary* defines *mascon* as "a concentration of dense matter below the moon's surface, with strong gravitational pull."

5. James Weldon Johnson, with his brother J. Rosamund Johnson, collected and edited two volumes of American Negro Spirituals.

6. The New Black Arts movement is the name given to the African American cultural movement that developed alongside the Black Power political movement. Lasting from about 1965 to 1975, the movement was rooted in a pan-African nationalist aesthetics, which posited a cultural unity of the African world.

CHAPTER 2: ORALITY

1. "Double consciousness" is a term used by W.E.B. Du Bois in *The Souls of Black Folk* to describe the state of African Americans, being both Black and American.

2. The "Amen Corner" is the name given to that part of the congregation that is most responsive to the words of the preacher and, by extension, to any individual or collective verbal encouragement or assent.

3. A public reading by a poet such as Gwendolyn Brooks, Amiri Baraka, Haki Madhubuti, or Sonia Sanchez before an African American audience is a communal language event. It is only in the 1990s that the printed words of the Last Poets, a group of poets who record and perform under that name, and Gil Scott Heron have become available to readers in book form.

4. "Simple" is the name Langston Hughes gives to his character Jess B. Semple, in a characteristically African American way of naming.

5. A term for African American vernacular speech first used around 1979, it reentered popular discourse in 1997 in a debate over how to teach reading and writing skills to African American children.

6. Although the poems of *God's Trombones* often are declaimed in an elocutionary fashion, such performers as Val Gray Ward utilize the singsong cadences of the traditional church in their performances.

7. A return to the mother tongue is often observable during times of heightened group consciousness or nationalism, such as during the Harlem Renaissance or the Black Arts movement. The mother tongue, too, seems to be uniquely suited during periods of struggle to communicate invective and insult directed toward an oppressor or enemy.

8. Stephen Henderson, Geneva Smitherman, and poet Carolyn Rodgers offer similar listings.

9. The poetry slam is a 1990s development in performance in which poets compete with each other before either a panel of judges or the entire audience to deliver the best performance of a poem. In music, jazz performers vie with each other to perform the best solo; rappers have extended the jazz tradition into their performances in what is known as cutting contests.

10. See the work of Amiri Baraka, Ishmael Reed, Haki Madhubuti, and the early

Carolyn Rodgers, Sonia Sanchez, and Nikki Giovanni. Women poets abandoned profanity before their male peers.

11. The word *lumpen,* taken from Karl Marx's term *Lumpenproletariat,* was used in the 1960s by the Black Panthers and others to refer to the masses of the poor and working class.

CHAPTER 3: THE POETRY OF PREACHMENT

1. The poem was set to music and retitled "Elegy" by Oscar Brown, Jr.
2. Brooks currently self-publishes or publishes and distributes through Haki Madhubuti's Third World Press.
3. The mourners' bench is the place in the traditional church where sinners sit before being called to profess faith and repentance.

CHAPTER FOUR: SONG/TALK

1. Andrew P. Watson provides an introductory essay, "Negro Primitive Religious Services," to a collection of oral conversion narratives and personal narratives of former slaves. The essay describes traditional religious services, including prayer and sermon. That the African American ceremonies are described by the same anthropological term, *primitive,* as are traditional African worship ceremonies, is suggestive.
2. Several of Shepp's recordings made in the 1960s and 1970s combine music and poetic recitations of his own work. The New Black Poetry was often accompanied by the New Black Music.
3. Riffing in the African American musical tradition is the jazz equivalent of worrying the line.
4. In a television special on gospel music broadcast during the early 1990s, Patti LaBelle recited the poem, remarking that she had recently lost relatives to cancer. She read from a pulpit like a singing preacher leading up to the next song.
5. By composer-musician Phil Cohran.
6. A few examples: Langston Hughes celebrated Duke, Count Basie, Dizzy Gillespie, and others in his poems. Amiri Baraka, Ted Joans, and Bob Kaufman celebrated jazz musicians, particularly Bird (Charlie Parker) and Charles Mingus during the Beat era. Amiri Baraka and Larry Neal acted as cultural godfathers to the New Black Arts movement through the publication of their anthology, *Black Fire,* which includes many musical tributes. Poets such as Haki Madhubuti, Nikki Giovanni, Etheridge Knight, and Sonia Sanchez wrote praise poems for African American musicians. Today poets such as Rita Dove, Yusef Komunyakaa, Patricia Smith, and Paul Beatty join the chorus of poets who incorporate musical references, allusions, subjects, and themes in their poems.

CHAPTER 5: TELL MY STORY

1. I remember in particular a game whose chant began, "This the way we billy billy" and went on to encourage its players to "strut Miss Sally". The game did for girls in body language what the boasts did for the boys in words. The implications of African American children's games are the subject for another book.

2. Women blues singers from Ma Rainey and Bessie Smith on have sung explicit statements of their power, particularly in the sexual sphere. Today, rappers such as Little Kim extend the trend of female raunchiness from these blues singers in the more explicit language of today. As the Carolyn Rodgers epigraph notes, "cussing in public" was one of the hallmarks of the "revolutionary" youth culture of the late 1960s and early 1970s. Taking the language of the streets into the concert hall and onto the poetry reading platform, New Black Arts singers and poets changed the standard for acceptable language. The songs do still get censored for radio play.

3. Both traditional Western attitudes toward women and nationalist pronouncements on the role of African women contrast with portraits of powerful women in both African American vernacular and intellectual discourse. The result is a mass of contradictory metaphors and tropes.

4. Though he does not make an appearance in the blockbuster film, in the toast tradition Shine, a menial laborer on the *Titanic*, was shoveling coal when that mighty ship sank. Despite tempting offers of sex, money, and salvation from white drowning passengers, "Shine swam on," and lived to tell the story.

5. Angela Davis also includes transcriptions of all extant lyrics of songs recorded by Rainey and Smith, many of which were their own compositions.

6. Novelist and playwright Alice Childress became so impatient with the implied responsibility of African American women for the "manhood" of African American men that she has a woman character in her play *Mojo* say of that precious commodity, "*I* didn't take it!"

7. Hull was speaking in 1977 at a seminar cosponsored by Yale University and the Modern Language Association. The seminar resulted in the MLA publication *The Reconstruction of Instruction*.

8. Examples are the off-Broadway production *A Hand Is on the Gate* in the sixties, the Kuumba Theater's ritual performances in Chicago during the seventies, and Ntozake Shange's "choreopoem" *For Colored Girls . . .*

CHAPTER 6: "BLACK IS . . . AND BLACK AIN'T"

1. "Dink's Song," as collected by Alan Lomax, has been recorded by Harry Belafonte among others.

2. Although the Greek myth is about male characters, the African American story has men, women, and children flying back "home" to Guinea or Africa.

3. As the great-grandaughter of the "mother" of Philadelphia Missionary Baptist Church, I am very familiar with the roles of women in the traditional church. My great-grandmother sat in the first row alongside the other

women leaders of the church, including the pastor's wife, and was often called on to lead the congregation in prayer and song.

4. Mari Evans was anthologized by Arna Bontemps and Langston Hughes in the early sixties; however, it was her 1970 collection *I Am a Black Woman* that announced her presence. Evans's association with *Negro Digest/ Black World* magazine cemented her identification with the New Black Arts movement.

5. I use "gay" to refer to gay male and "lesbian" to refer to gay female.

6. Afrikete is the name Audre Lorde gives to her goddess figure.

7. Joseph Beam, Essex Hemphill, and Melvin Dixon are deceased.

8. American culture in general and African American culture in particular seem to find less difficulty in reading and listening to lesbians than to gay men. Ideas and feelings about maleness and masculinity resist inclusion of such difference.

Works Cited

Abrahams, Roger D. *Deep Down in the Jungle: Negro Narrative Folklore from the Streets of Philadelphia.* Chicago: Aldine, 1970.

———. "Joking: The Training of the Man of Words in Talking Broad," in Kochman, *Rappin,'* 215–240.

———, and John F. Szwed, eds. *After Africa.* New Haven, Conn.: Yale University Press, 1983.

Adoff, Arnold, ed. *The Poetry of Black America: Anthology of the 20th Century.* New York: Harper and Row, 1973.

Algarin, Miguel, and Bob Holman, eds.*Aloud: Voices from the Nuyorican Poets Cafe.* New York: McRae-Holt, 1994.

Alexander, Elizabeth. "Narrative: Ali," in Harper and Walton, 310–316.

Amini, Johari. *Let's Go Some Where.* Chicago: Third World Press, 1970.

Asante, Molefi Kete. *African and African American Communication Continuities.* CIS Special Studies #61. Buffalo: State University of New York Press, 1975

———. *The Afrocentric Idea.* Philadelphia: Temple University Press, 1987.

Asim, Jabari. "Hip Hop Bop," in Powell and Baraka, *In the Tradition,* 55–56.

Baker, Houston A. Jr. *Black Studies, Rap and the Academy.* Chicago: University of Chicago Press, 1984.

———. *Blues, Ideology, and Afro-American Literature.* Chicago: University of Chicago Press, 1994.

Baraka, Amiri (LeRoi Jones). *Black Magic: Poetry: 1961–1967.* New York: Bobbs-Merrill, 1969.

———. *Black Music.* New York: Quill, 1967.

———. *Selected Poetry.* New York: Morrow, 1979.

Barksdale, Richard K. "Margaret Walker: Folk Orature and Historical Prophecy." In *Black American Poets between Worlds, 1940–960,* edited by R. Baxter Miller. Knoxville: University of Tennessee Press, 1986. 104–117.

Beam, Joseph, ed. *In the Life: A Black Gay Anthology.* Boston: Alyson Publishing Company, 1986.

Blount, Marcellus. "The Preacherly Text: African American Poetry and Vernacular Performance." *PMLA* 107 (May 1992): 582–593.

Brooks, Gwendolyn. *Beckonings.* Detroit: Broadside Press, 1975.

———. *Blacks.* Chicago: Third World Press, 1987.

———. *Children Coming Home.* Chicago: David Press, 1991.

————. *Winnie.* Chicago: David Press, 1988.

Brown, H. Rap. "Street Talk" in Kochman, *Rappin',* 205–208.

Brown, Sterling A. *The Collected Poems of Sterling A. Brown,* Selected by Michael S. Harper. The National Poetry Series. Chicago: Harper Colophon, 1983.

————. *The Last Ride of Wild Bill.* Detroit: Broadside Press, 1975.

————. *Negro Poetry and Drama and the Negro in American Fiction.* 1937. Reprint, New York: Atheneum, 1969.

Calt, Stephen. "The Country Blues as Meaning." In Grossman, Grossman, and Calt, 8–35.

Cortez, Jayne. *Coagulations: New and Selected Poems.* New York: Thunder's Mouth Press, 1984.

Dance, Daryl Cumber. *Shuckin' and Jivin': Folklore from Contemporary Black Americans.* Bloomington: University of Indiana Press, 1978.

Davis, Angela. *Blues Legacies and Black Feminism: Gertrude "Ma" Rainey, Bessie Smith, and Billie Holiday.* New York: Random House, 1998.

Dillard, J. L. *Black English: Its History and Usage in the United States.* New York: Vintage, 1973.

Dunbar, Paul Laurence. *The Collected Poetry.* Edited with an Introduction by Joanne Braxton. Charlottesville: University of Virginia Press, 1993.

Dundes, Alan, ed. *Mother Wit from the Laughing Barrel: Readings in the Interpretation of Afro-American Folklore.* Jackson: University of Mississippi Press, 1990.

Evans, Mari. *I Am a Black Woman.* New York: Morrow, 1970.

————. *Nightstar, 1973–78.* Los Angeles: Center for Afro-American Studies, UCLA, 1981.

Fernando, S. H. Jr. *The New Beats: Exploring the Music, Culture, and Attitudes of Hip—Hop.* New York: Doubleday-Anchor, 1994.

Finnegan, Ruth. *Oral Poetry: Its Nature, Significance and Social Context.* Cambridge: Cambridge University Press, 1977.

Fisher, Dexter, and Robert B. Stepto, eds. *Afro-American .Literature: The Reconstruction of Instruction.* New York: Modern Language Association, 1979.

Folk Blues. New York: Arc Music, 1965.

Gaines, Reg E. "Please Don't Take My Air Jordans," in Algarin and Holman, 85–87.

Gates, Henry Louis Jr. *The Signifying Monkey: A Theory of African-American Literary Criticism.* New York: Oxford University Press, 1988.

George, Nelson. *Buppies, B-Boys, Baps and Bohos: Notes on Post-Soul Black Culture.* New York: HarperCollins, 1992.

Gibson, Donald B., ed. *Modern Black Poets: A Collection of Critical Essays.* Englewood Cliffs, N.J.: Prentice Hall, 1973.

Gilbert, Derrick I. M. (a.k.a. D-Knowledge), ed. *Catch the Fire!!!: A Cross-Generational Anthology of Contemporary African-American Poetry.* New York: Riverhead, 1998.

Gilroy, Paul. *The Black Atlantic: Modernity and Double Consciousness.* Cambridge, Mass.: Harvard University Press, 1993.

Giovanni, Nikki. *Black Feeling, Black Talk.* Detroit: Broadside Press, 1970.

————. *Re: Creation.* Detroit: Broadside Press, 1970.

Grossman, Stefan, Hal Grossman, and Stephen Calt, eds. *Country Blues Songbook.* New York: Oak Books, 1973.

Harper, Michael S. Interview in *American Poetry Observed: Poets on Their Work,* edited by Joe David Bellamy. Urbana: University of Illinois Press, 1984, 88–100.

————, **and Anthony Walton,** eds. *Every Shut Eye Ain't Asleep: An Anthology of Poetry by African Americans Since 1945.* Boston: Little Brown, 1994.

Haslam, Gerald W. *Afro-American Oral Literature.* New York: Harper and Row, 1975.

Hayden, Robert. *Collected Poems.* Edited by Frederick Glaysher. New York: Liveright, 1985.

Hemphill, Essex. "The Tomb of Sorrow," in *Brother to Brother,* 75–83.

————, ed. *Brother to Brother: New Writings by Black Gay Men.* Conceived by Joseph Beam. Boston: Alyson Publishing Company, 1991.

Henderson, Stephen. *Understanding the New Black Poetry: Black Speech and Black Music as Poetic References.* New York: Morrow, 1973.

Hogue, W. Lawrence. *Discourse and the Other: The Production of the Afro-American Text.* Durham, N.C.: Duke University Press, 1986.

————. *Race, Modernity, Postmodernity: A Look at the History of the Literature of People of Color Since the 1960's.* Albany: State University of New York Press, 1996.

Holt, Grace Sims. "'Inversion' in Black Communication," in Kochman, *Rappin',* 152–159.

————. "Stylin' outta the black pulpit," in Kochman, *Rappin',* 189–204.

Honey, Maureen, ed. *Shadowed Dreams: Women's Poetry of the Harlem Renaissance.* New Brunswick, N.J.: Rutgers University Press, 1989.

Howard-Pitney, David. *The Afro-American Jeremiad: Appeals for Justice in America.* Philadelphia: Temple University Press, 1990.

Hubbard, Dolan. *The Sermon and the African American Literary Imagination.* Columbus: University of Missouri Press, 1994.

Hughes, Langston. *Complete Poems.* Edited by Arnold Rampersad. New York: Knopf, 1994.

Jackson, Bruce, ed. *"Get Your Ass in the Water and Swim Like Me": Narrative Poetry from Black Oral Tradition.* Cambridge: Harvard University Press, 1974.

Jeffers, Lance. *When I Know the Beauty of My Black Hand.* Detroit: Broadside Press, 1974.

Johnson, Clifton H., and Paul Radin, eds. *God Struck Me Dead: Religious Conversion Experiences and Autobiographies of Ex-Slaves.* New York: Pilgrim Press, 1969.

Johnson, James Weldon. *God's Trombones: Seven Negro Sermons in Verse.* New York: Viking Compass, 1927. Reprint, 1969.

———. "Preface," *God's Trombones,* 1–11.

———, ed. *The Book of American Negro Poetry.* New York: Harcourt, 1922. Rev. ed., 1931.

Jones, Gayl. *Liberating Voices: Oral Tradition in African American Literature.* Cambridge: Harvard University Press, 1991.

Jones, Patricia Spears. *The Weather That Kills.* Minneapolis, Minn.: Coffee House Press, 1995.

Jordan, June. *Naming Our Destiny: New and Selected Poems.* New York: Thunder's Mouth Press, 1989.

———. *Things That I Do in the Dark: Selected Poems.* New York: Random House, 1977.

Joyce, Joyce Ann. *Warriors, Conjurors and Priests: Defining African-Centered Literary Criticism.* Chicago: Third World Press, 1994.

Katz, Bernard, ed. *The Social Implications of Early Negro Music in the United States.* New York: Arno, 1969.

Knight, Etheridge. *The Essential Etheridge Knight.* Pittsburgh, Pa.: University of Pittsburgh Press, 1986.

Kochman, Thomas. "Toward an Ethnography of Black American Speech Behavior," in *Rappin',* 241–264.

Kochman, Thomas, ed. *Rappin' and Stylin' Out: Communication in Urban Black America.* Urbana: University of Illinois Press, 1972.

Krehbiel, Henry Edward. *Afro-American Folksongs: A Study in Racial and National Music,* 1914. New York: Frederick Ungar, 1962.

Labov, William, Paul Cohen, Clarence Robins, and John Lewis. "Toasts," in Dundes, 329–347.

Lorde, Audre. *Chosen Poems—Old and New.* New York, Norton, 1982.

Madhubuti, Haki R. (Don L. Lee). *Directionscore: Selected and New Poems.* Detroit: Broadside Press, 1971.

———. *We Walk the Way of the New World.* Detroit: Broadside Press, 1970.

Major, Clarence. *Jubu to Jive: A Dictionary of African-American Slang.* New York: Penguin, 1994.

Melheim, D. H. *Gwendolyn Brooks: Poetry and the Heroic Voice.* Lexington: University Press of Kentucky, 1987.

————. *Heroism in the New Black Poetry: Introduction and Interviews.* Lexington: University Press of Kentucky, 1990.

Melnick, Mimi Clar. "I Can Peep through Muddy Water & Spy Dry Land: Boasts in the Blues," in Dundes, 267–276.

Miller, R. Baxter, ed. *Black American Poets Between Worlds, 1940–1960.* Knoxville: University of Tennessee Press, 1986.

Mitchell-Kernan, Claudia. "Signifying, loud-talking and marking," in Kochman, *Rappin'*, 315–335.

Murray, Albert. *The Omni-Americans: New Perspectives on Black Experience and American Culture.* New York: Discus, 1970.

————. *Stomping the Blues.* New York: McGraw-Hill, 1976.

Neal, Larry. *Visions of a Liberated Future: Black Arts Movement Writings.* Edited by Michael Schwartz. New York: Thunder's Mouth Press, 1989.

Nelson, Havelock , and Michael A. Gonzalez. *Bring the Noise: A Guide to Rap Music and Hip Hop Culture.* New York: Harmony, 1991.

Nielsen, Aldon Lynn. *Black Chant: Languages of African-American Postmodernism.* Cambridge: Cambridge University Press, 1997.

Ong, Walter J. *Orality and Literacy: The Technologizing of the Word.* London: Routledge, 1982.

Powell, Kevin, and Ras Baraka, eds. *In the Tradition: An Anthology of Young Black Writers.* New York: Harlem River Books, 1992.

Randall, Dudley, and Margaret G. Burroughs, eds. *For Malcolm: Poems on the Life and the Death of Malcolm X.* Detroit: Broadside Press, 1969.

Redmond, Eugene. *Drumvoices: The Mission of Afro-American Poetry.* Garden City, N.Y.: Anchor, 1975.

Reed, Ishmael. *catechism of d neoamerican hoodoo church.* London: Paul Bremen, 1971.

Rodgers, Carolyn M. "Black Poetry—Where It's At," in Kochman, *Rappin'*, 336–345.

————. *How I Got Ovah.* New York: Doubleday/Anchor, 1976.

————. *Songs of a Black Bird.* Chicago: Third World Press, 1969.

Rohlehr, Gordon. "The Shape of that Hurt." In *Voiceprint: An Anthology of Oral and Related Poetry from the Caribbean,* selected and edited by Stewart Brown, Merwyn Morris, and Gordon Rohlehr. Harlow, U.K.: Longman, 1989. 1–23.

Roscoe, Adrian A. *Mother Is Gold: A Study in West African Literature.* Cambridge: Cambridge University Press, 1971.

Rose, Tricia. *Black Noise: Rap Music and Black Culture in Contemporary America.* Hanover, N.H.: Wesleyan-New England, 1994.

Rosenberg, Bruce A. *The Art of the American Folk Preacher.* New York: Oxford University Press, 1970.

Rushin, Kate. *The Black Back—Ups: Poetry.* Ithaca, N.Y.: Firebrand Books, 1993.

Saloy, Mona Lisa. *The "N Word": A Monograph.* New Orleans, La.: Black Bayou, 1994.

Sanchez, Sonia. Interview, in Gilbert, 221–224.

———. *I've Been a Woman: New and Selected Poems.* Sausalito, Calif.: Black Scholar Press, 1978.

Schipper, Mineke. *Beyond the Boundaries: African Literature and Literary Theory.* London: Allison and Busby, 1985.

Sexton, Adam, ed. *Rap on Rap: Straight-up Talk on Hip Hop Culture.* New York: Delta,1995

Simmons, Judith Dothard. *Judith's Blues.* Detroit: Broadside Press Press, 1973.

Smith, Patricia. *Life According to Motown.* Chicago: Tia Chucha, 1991.

Smitherman, Geneva. *Black Language and Culture: Sounds of Soul.* New York: Harper, 1975.

———. *Black Talk: Words and Phrases from the Hood to the Amen Corner.* Boston: Houghton Mifflin, 1994.

Stetson, Erlene, ed. *Black Sister: Poetry by Black American Women, 1746–1980.* Bloomington: Indiana University Press, 1981.

Stewart, Garrett. *Reading Voices: Literature and the Phonotext.* Berkeley: University of California Press, 1990.

Tate, Greg. *Flyboy in the Buttermilk: Essays on Contemporary America.* New York: Simon and Schuster, 1992.

Walker, Margaret. *This Is My Century: New and Collected Poems.* Athens: University of Georgia Press, 1989.

Watson, Andrew P. "Negro Primitive Religious Services," in C. Johnson, 1–12.

Williams, Sherley Anne. "The Blues Roots of Contemporary Afro-American Poetry," in Fisher and Stepto, 72–87.

DISCOGRAPHY

Brown, Oscar, Jr. "Signifyin' Monkey," *Sin & Soul.* LP. Columbia, 1973.

Cole, Nat. "Straighten Up and Fly Right," *The Best of the Nat King Cole Trio: Vocal Classics (1942–46).* CD. Capitol, 1995.

Get Your Ass in the Water and Swim Like Me: Narrative Poetry from Black Oral Tradition, **recorded and edited by Bruce Jackson. LP. Rounder, 1976.**

Grandmaster Flash and the Furious Five. "The Message." LP. Sugar Hill, 1982.

James, Willis. *Afro American Music,* with accompanying text. LP. Arch Records #AA702, 1970.

Queen Latifah (Dana Owens). "Ladies First" with Monie Love, *All Hail the Queen.* Audiocassette. Tommy Boy, 1989.

————."U.N.I.T.Y.," *Black Reign.* CD. Motown, 1993.

————. "Woman for the Job," *Silent Assassin,* Sly & Robbie. CD. Island, 1989.

Taylor, Koko. *The Earthshaker.* LP. Alligator, 1978.

ORAL SOURCES

References to oral literature are drawn from memory, not from written sources.

Bibliography

In 1965, when I was a young graduate student at Loyola University in Chicago, I decided that my project for a course in research methodology and bibliography would be a compilation of criticism on African American poetry published between 1920 and 1960. I was interested in determining the amount and nature of the critical resources available on the writers I wished to make the subject of my dissertation. I was preparing myself, I thought at the time, to declare a concentration in modern American poetry and to write a dissertation on African American poetry. A semester of research yielded one of the smallest bibliographies in the class. Most of the critical material I did find had appeared in "popular" journals such as *Crisis* and *Negro Digest,* later to become *Black World.* It is somewhat dismaying to determine some thirty years later that, although the list of poets and their works has multiplied exponentially, in comparison to criticism on narrative the amount of criticism on poetry remains meager. This bibliography is somewhat idiosyncratic in that it represents what I own or have read. It is, however, fairly exhaustive. For ease of reference, I have divided it into the following sections: Poetry Anthologies; Literature Anthologies; Music Books; The Poets; Criticism, Books; Criticism, Articles and Essays; and Recorded Poetry.

POETRY ANTHOLOGIES

Abdul, Raoul, ed. *The Magic of Black Poetry.* New York: Dodd, Mead, 1972.

Adoff, Arnold, ed. *I Am the Darker Brother: An Anthology of Modern Poems by Negro Americans.* New York: Macmillan, 1968.

———. *Black Out Loud: An Anthology of Modern Poems by Black Americans.* New York: Macmillan, 1972.

———. *The Poetry of Black Americans: Anthology of the Twentieth Century.* With an Introduction by Gwendolyn Brooks. New York: Harper, 1973.

Algarin, Miguel, and Bob Holman, eds. *Aloud: Voices from the Nuyorican Café.* New York: McRae-Holt, 1994. A multiracial anthology.

Bontemps, Arna, ed. *American Negro Poetry.* Rev. ed. New York: Hill and Wang, 1973.

———. comp. *Golden Slippers: An Anthology of Negro Poetry for Young Readers.* New York: Harper and Row, 1941.

Bremen, Paul, ed. *You Better Believe It: Black Verse in English from Africa, the West Indies and the United States.* Selected and annotated. New York: Penguin, 1973.

Brooks, Gwendolyn, ed. *A Broadside Treasury.* Detroit: Broadside, 1971.

Coombs, Orde, ed. *We Speak as Liberators: Black Young Poets.* New York: Dodd, Mead, 1970.

Cullen, Countee, ed. *Caroling Dusk: An Anthology of Verse by Negro Poets.* New York: Harper and Row, 1927.

Feinstein, Sascha, and Yusef Komunyakaa, eds. *The Jazz Poetry Anthology.* Bloomington: Indiana University Press, 1991. A multiracial anthology.

Gilbert, Derrick I. M. (a.k.a. D-Knowledge), ed. *Catch the Fire!!! : A Cross-Generational Anthology of Contemporary African-American Poetry.* New York: Riverhead, 1998.

Harper, Michael S., and Anthony Walton, eds. *Every Shut Eye Ain't Asleep: An* Anthology of Poetry by African Americans Since 1945. *Boston: Little, Brown, 1994.*

Hayden, Robert, ed. *Kaleidoscope: Poems by American Negro Poets.* With an introduction by the ed. New York: Harcourt, 1967.

Henderson, Stephen B., ed. *Understanding the New Black Poetry: Black Speech and Black Music as Poetic References.* New York: William Morrow, 1973.

Honey, Maureen, ed. *Shadowed Dreams: Women's Poetry of the Harlem Renaissance.* New Brunswick, N.J.: Rutgers University Press, 1989.

Hughes, Langston, ed. *New Negro Poets: USA.* Foreword by Gwendolyn Brooks. Bloomington: Indiana University Press, 1964.

Hughes, Langston, and Arna Bontemps, eds. *The Poetry of the Negro: 1746–1970.* Garden City, N.Y.: Anchor-Doubleday, 1970.

Johnson, James Weldon, ed. *The Book of American Negro Poetry.* Rev. ed. New York: Harcourt, 1931.

Jordan, June. *Soulscript.* Garden City, N.Y.: Zenith/ Doubleday, 1970.

King, Woodie, ed. *Black Spirits: A Festival of New Black Poets in America.* With Artistic Consultant Imamu Amiri Baraka. Foreword by Nikki Giovanni. Introduction by Don L. Lee. New York: Random House, 1972.

Madgett, Naommi Long, ed. *A Milestone Sampler: Fifteenth Anniversary Anthology.* Detroit: Lotus Press, 1988.

Major, Clarence, ed. *The New Black Poetry.* New York: International, 1969.

————. *The Garden Thrives: Twentieth-Century African-American Poetry.* With an introduction by the editor. New York: HarperCollins, 1996.

Miller, Adam David, ed. *Dices or Black Bones: Black Voices of the Seventies.* Boston: Houghton Mifflin, 1970.

Miller, E. Ethelbert, ed. *In Search of Color Everywhere: A Collection of African-American Poetry.* New York: Stewart, Tabori and Chang, 1994.

Patterson, Lindsay, ed. *A Rock Against the Wind: African American Poems and Letters of Love and Passion.* With a Foreword by Ruby Dee. New York: Perigee, 1996.

Pool, Rosey E., ed. *Beyond the Blues: New Poems by American Negroes.* With an introduction by the editor. Chester Springs, Pa.: Dufour, 1962.

Randall, Dudley, ed. *The Black Poets.* New York: Bantam, 1971.

————, and Margaret G. Burroughs, eds. *For Malcolm: Poems on the Life and the Death of Malcolm X.* Detroit: Broadside, 1969.

Robinson, William H., ed. *Early Black American Poets: Selections with Biographical and Critical Introductions.* Dubuque, Iowa: Brown, 1971.

Stetson, Erlene, ed. *Black Sister: Poetry by Black American Women, 1746–1980.* Bloomington: Indiana University Press, 1981.

Ward, Jerry W., Jr., ed. *Trouble the Waters: 250 Years of African-American Poetry.* With an introduction by the editor. New York: Mentor, 1997.

Wilentz, Ted, and Tom Weatherly, eds. *Natural Process: An Anthology of New Black Poetry.* New York: Hill and Wang, 1970.

LITERATURE ANTHOLOGIES

Alhamisi, Ahmad, and Harun Kofi Wangara, eds. *Black Art: An Anthology of Black Creations.* Detroit: Black Arts, 1969.

Baker, Houston A., Jr., ed. *Black Literature in America.* New York: McGraw-Hill, 1971.

Baraka, Amiri (LeRoi Jones), and Amina Baraka, eds. *Confirmation: An Anthology of African American Women.* New York: Quill, 1983.

Barksdale, Richard, and Keneth Kinnamon, eds. *Black Writers of America: A Comprehensive Anthology.* New York: Macmillan, 1972.

Beam, Joseph, ed. *In the Life: A Black Gay Anthology.* Boston: Alyson, 1986.

Brooks, Gwendolyn, ed. *Jump Bad: An Anthology of the Gwendolyn Brooks Writers Workshop.* Detroit: Broadside, 1971.

Brown, Sterling A., Arthur P. Davis, and Ulysses Lee, eds. *The Negro Caravan.* 1941. Repr., New York: Arno, 1969.

Chambers, Bradford, and Rebecca Moon, eds. *Right On! An Anthology of Black Literature.* New York: New American Liberary, 1970.

Chapman, Abraham, ed. *Black Voices: An Anthology of Afro-American Literature.* New York: Mentor, 1968.

————. *New Black Voices.* New York: Mentor, 1972.

Davis, Arthur P., J. Saunders Redding, and Joyce Ann Joyce, eds. *The New Cavalcade.* Washington, D.C.: Howard University Press, 1992.

Davis, Charles T., and Daniel Walden, eds. *On Being Black: Writings by Afro-Americans from Frederick Douglass to the Present.* New York: Fawcett, 1970.

Donalson, Melvin, ed. *Cornerstones: An Anthology of African American Literature.* New York: St. Martin's, 1996.

Emanuel, James A., and Theodore L. Gross, eds. *Dark Symphony: Negro Literature in America.* New York: Free Press, 1968.

Freedman, Frances S., ed. *The Black American Experience: A New Anthology of Black Literature.* New York: Bantam, 1970.

Gates, Henry Louis, and Nellie McKay, eds. *The Norton Anthology of African American Literature*. New York: Norton, 1996.

Harper, Michael S., and Robert B. Stepto, eds. *Chant of Saints: A Gathering of Afro-American Literature, Art, and Scholarship*. Urbana: University of Illinois Press, 1979.

Hayden, Robert, David J. Burrow, and Frederick R. Lapides, eds. *Afro-American Literature: An Introduction*. New York: Harcourt, 1971.

Hemphill, Essex, ed. *Brother to Brother: New Writings by Black Gay Men*. Conceived by Joseph Fairchild Beam. Boston: Alyson, 1991.

Iman, Yusef, ed. *Afro-Arts Anthology*. Newark, N.J.: Jihad, 1966.

Jones, LeRoi (Amiri Baraka), and Larry Neal, eds. *Black Fire: An Anthology of Afro-American Writing*. New York: William Morrow, 1968.

Lange, Art, and Nathaniel Mackey, eds. *Moment's Notice: Jazz in Poetry and Prose*. Minneapolis, Minn.: Coffee House Press, 1993. A Multicultural Anthology.

Locke, Alain, ed. *The New Negro*. 1925. New York: Atheneum, 1969.

Long, Richard A., and Eugenia W. Collier, eds. *Afro-American Writing: An Anthology of Afro-American Prose and Poetry*. Philadelphia: University of Pennsylvania Press, 1985.

McKinley, Catherine E., and L. Joyce Delaney, eds. *Afrikete*. Garden City, N.Y.: Anchor-Doubleday, 1995.

Miller, Ruth, ed. *Blackamerican Literature: 1760–Present*. New York: Glencoe, 1971.

Mullane, Deidre, ed. *Crossing the Danger Water: Three Hundred Years of African-American Writing*. Garden City, N.Y.: Anchor-Doubleday, 1993.

Murray, Alma, and Robert Thomas, eds. *Major Black Writers*. New York: Scholastic, 1971.

Nommo 2: Remembering Ourselves Whole: An OBAC Anthology of Contemporary Black Writing. Chicago: OBAhouse, 1990.

Parks, Carole A., ed. *Nommo: A Literary Legacy of Black Chicago (1967–1987)*. Chicago: OBAhouse, 1987.

Powell, Kevin, and Ras Baraka, eds. *In the Tradition: An Anthology of Young Black Writers*. New York: Harlem River, 1992.

Randall, Dudley, ed. *Homage to Hoyt Fuller*. Detroit: Broadside, 1984.

Roses, Lorraine Elena, and Ruth Elizabeth Randolph, eds. *Harlem's Glory: Black Women Writing 1900–1950*. Cambridge: Harvard University Press, 1996.

Sherman, Joan R., ed. *African American Poetry: An Anthology, 1773–1927*. Mineola, NY: Dover Publications, 1997.

Shockley, Ann Allen, ed. *Afro-American Women Writers, 1746–1933: An Anthology and Critical Guide*. New York: Meridan-NAL, 1988.

Simmons, Gloria M., and Helene D. Hutchinson, eds. *Black Culture: Reading and Writing Black*. New York: Holt, 1972.

Stanford, Barbara Dods, ed. *I, Too, Sing America: Black Voices in American Literature.* New York: Hayden, 1971.

Troupe, Quincy, and Rainer Schulte, eds. *Giant Talk: An Anthology of Third World Writings.* New York: Vintage, 1975.

Turner, Darwin T., ed. *Black American Literataure: Essays, Poetry, Ficition, Drama.* New York: Merrill, 1970.

Turner, Faythe, ed. *Puerto Rican Writers at Home in the USA: An Anthology.* New York: Open Hand, 1991.

Williams, John A., ed. *Beyond the Angry Black.* New York: NAL, 1971.

Young, Al, ed. *African American Literature: A Brief Introduction and Anthology.* New York: HarperCollins, 1996.

MUSIC BOOKS

Folk Blues. New York: Arc Music, 1965.

Grossman, Stefan, Hal Grossman, and Stephen Calt, eds. *Country Blues Songbook.* New York: Oak, 1973.

THE POETS

Addison, Lloyd. *The Aura and the Umbra.* London: Paul Bremen, 1970.

Ai. *Cruelty.* Boston: Houghton Mifflin, 1979.

———. *Fate: New Poems.* Boston: Houghton Mifflin, 1991.

———. *Greed.* New York: Norton, 1993.

———. *Killing Floor.* Boston: Houghton Mifflin, 1979.

———. *Sin: Poems.* Boston: Houghton Mifflin, 1986.

Alexander, Elizabeth. *The Venus Hottentot.* Charlottesville: University of Virginia Press, 1990.

Alhamisi, Ahmed Akinwole. *Guerilla Warfare.* Detroit: Black Arts, 1970.

———. *Holy Ghosts.* Detroit: Broadside, 1972.

Allen, Samuel. *Every Round and Other Poems.* Detroit: Lotus Press, 1987.

———. *Paul Vesey's Ledger.* Heritage, 27. London: Paul Bremen, 1975.

Amini, Johari (Jewel C. Latimore). *Black Essence.* Chicago: Third World Press, 1968.

———. *A Folk Fable.* Chicago: Third World Press, 1969.

———. *Images in Black.* Chicago: Third World Press, 1969.

———. *Let's Go Some Where.* Chicago: Third World Press, 1969.

Angelou, Maya. *Complete Collected Poems.* New York: Random House, 1994.

———. *And Still I Rise.* New York: Random House, 1978.

———. *I Shall Not Be Moved.* New York: Random House, 1990.

———. *Just Give a Cool Drink of Water . . . 'Fore I Diiie.* New York: Random House, 1971.

————. *Oh Pray My Wings Are Gonna Fit Me Well.* New York: Random House, 1975.

————. *Shaker, Why Don't You Sing?* New York: Random House, 1983.

Atkins, Russel. *Heretofore.* London: Paul Bremen, 1968.

Aubert, Alvin. *Against the Blues.* Detroit: Broadside, 1972.

————. *Winter Comes: Collected Poems, 1967–1992.* Pittsburgh, Pa.: Carnegie-Mellon University Press, 1994.

Baraka, Amiri (LeRoi Jones). *Black Magic: Poetry 1962–1967.* New York: Bobbs Merrill, 1967. First book published as Baraka.

Baraka, Amiri. *The Dead Lecturer.* New York: Grove, 1964.

————. *In Our Terribleness.* New York: Bobbs-Merrill, 1970.

————. *It's Nation Time.* Chicago: Third World Press, 1970.

————. *Preface to a Twenty-Volume Suicide Note.* New York: Totem, 1961.

————. *Selected Poetry.* New York: William Morrow, 1979.

————. *Spirit Reach.* Newark: Jihad, 1972.

————. *Transbluesency: The Selected Poems (1961–1995).* Edited by Paul Vangelisti. New York: Marsilio, 1995.

Barlow, George. *Gabriel.* Detroit: Broadside, 1974.

————. *Gumbo.* Garden City, N.Y.: Doubleday, 1981.

Barrax, Gerald. *Another Kind of Rain.* Pittsburgh: Pittsburgh University Press, 1970.

————. *An Audience of One.* Athens: University of Georgia Press, 1980.

————. *The Deaths of Animals and Other Gods.* Lexington: University of Kentucky Press, 1984.

Beatty, Paul. *Big Bank Take Little Bank.* New York: Nuyorican Poets Café, 1991.

————. *Joker, Joker, Deuce.* New York: Penguin, 1994.

Birch, McLane. *The Kandi Man.* Detroit: Broadside, 1975.

Blakely, Henry. *Windy Place.* Detroit: Broadside, 1974.

Bontemps, Arna. *Personals.* Heritage 4. London: Paul Bremen, 1973.

Boyd, Melba Joyce. *The Inventory of Black Roses.* Detroit: Past Tents, 1989.

————. *Thirteen Frozen Flamingos.* Bremen, Germany: Die Certal, 1984.

Boze, Arthur. *Black Words.* Detroit: Broadside, 1972.

Bragg, Linda Brown. *A Love Song to Black Men.* Detroit: Broadside, 1974.

Braxton, Joanne. *Sometimes I Think of Maryland.* Carbondale: Southern Illinois University Press, 1993.

Brooks, Gwendolyn. *Aloneness: A Children's Poem.* Detroit: Broadside, 1971

————. *Annie Allen.* New York: Harper and Row, 1949.

————. *The Bean Eaters.* New York: Harper and Row, 1960.

————. *Beckonings.* Detroit: Broadside, 1975.

————. *Black Love.* Chicago: Brooks, 1980.

————. *Blacks.* Chicago: Third World Press, 1987. Collected poems to 1968; selected poems to 1986.

————. *Bronzeville Boys and Girls.* New York: Harper and Row, 1955.

————. *Children Coming Home.* Chicago: David Press, 1991.

————. *Family Pictures.* Detroit: Broadside, 1970.

————. *Gottschalk and the Grande Tarantelle.* Chicago: David Press, 1988.

————. *In the Mecca.* New York: Harper and Row, 1968.

————. *The Near Johannesburg Boy and Other Poems.* Chicago: David Press, 1986.

————. *Primer for Blacks.* Chicago: Brooks, 1980.

————. *Riot.* Detroit: Broadside, 1969.

————. *Selected Poems.* New York: Harper and Row, 1963.

————. *A Street in Bronzeville.* New York: Harper and Row, 1945.

————. *To Disembark.* Chicago: Third World Press, 1981. Includes poems from *Riot, Family Pictures,* and *Beckonings,* along with new poems.

————. *Winnie.* Chicago: David Press, 1988.

————. *The World of Gwendolyn Brooks.* New York: Harper and Row, 1971. Collected works to 1968.

Brown, Sterling A. *The Collected Poems.* Selected by Michael S. Harper. New York: Harper, 1983.

————. *The Last Ride of Wild Bill.* Detroit: Broadside, 1975.

————. *Southern Road.* New York: Harcourt, 1932.

Burroughs, Margaret T. G. *What Shall I Tell My Children Who Are Black?* Chicago: Museum of African American History, 1968.

Butts, Anthony. *Fifth Season: Poems.* Kalamazoo: Western Michigan University Press, 1997.

Cannon, C. E. *Nigger.* Detroit: Broadside, 1972.

Chase-Riboud, Barbara. *Portrait of a Nude Woman as Cleopatra.* New York: William Morrow, 1987.

Clarke, Cheryl. *Experimental Love.* Ithaca, N.Y.: Firebrand, 1993.

Clarke, John Henrik. *Rebellion in Rhyme: The Early Poetry.* Trenton, N.J.: Africa World, 1991.

Clifton, Lucille. *The Book of Light.* Port Townsend, Wash.: Copper Canyon Press, 1993.

————. *Good News About the Earth.* New York: Random House, 1972.

————. *Good Times.* New York: Random House, 1969.

————. *good woman: poems and a memoir 1969–1980.* Brockport, N.Y.: BOA Editions, 1991.

————. *Next: New Poems.* Brockport, N.Y.: BOA Editions, 1987.

————. *An Ordinary Woman.* New York: Random House, 1974.

————. *Quilting: Poems 1987–1990.* Brockport, N.Y.: BOA Editions, 1991.

————. *two-headed woman.* Amherst: University of Massachusetts Press, 1980.

Clinton, Michelle T. *Good Sense and the Faithless.* Albuquerque: West End, 1994.

Cobb, Charlie. *Everywhere Is Yours.* Chicago: Third World Press, 1971.

Coleman, Wanda. *African Sleeping Sickness: Stories and Poems.* Santa Rosa, Calif.: Black Sparrow, 1990.

————. *Hand Dance.* Santa Rosa, Calif.: Black Sparrow, 1993.

————. *Heavy Daughter Blues.* Santa Rosa, Calif.: Black Sparrow, 1987.

————. *Imagos.* Santa Rosa, Calif.: Black Sparrow, 1983.

————. *Mad Dog Black Lady.* Santa Rosa, Calif.: Black Sparrow, 1979.

Cortez, Jayne. *Coagulations: New and Selected Poems.* New York: Thunder's Mouth, 1984.

————. *Festivals and Funerals.* New York: Bola, 1971.

————. *Firespitter.* New York: Bola, 1982.

————. *Mouth on Paper.* New York: Bola, 1977.

————. *Pissstained Stairs and the Monkey Man's Wares.* New York: Phrase Text, 1969.

————. *Scarifications.* New York: Bola, 1973.

Crouch, Stanley. *Ain't No Ambulances for No Nigguhs Tonight.* New York: Barron, 1972.

Cruz, Victor Hernandez. *Mainland.* New York: Random House, 1973.

————. *Red Beans.* Minneapolis, Minn.: Coffee House Press, 1991.

————. *Rhythm, Content and Flavor.* Houston, Tex.: Arte Publico, 1989.

————. *Snaps.* New York: Random House, 1969.

————. *Tropicalizations.* Berkeley, Calif.: Reed, Cannon and Johnson, 1976.

Cullen, Countee. *On These I Stand.* New York: Harper and Row, 1947.

————. *My Soul's High Song: The Collected Writings of Countee Cullen, Voice of the Harlem Renaissance.* Edited with an introduction by Gerald Early. Garden City, N.Y.: Doubleday, 1991.

Cuney, William Waring. *Storefront Church.* Heritage 23. London: Paul Bremen, 1973.

Damali (Denise Burnett). *I Am That We May Be.* Chicago: Third World Press, 1974.

Danner, Margaret. *The Down on a Thistle: Selected Poems, Prose Poems, and Songs.* Introduction by Samuel Allen. Afterword by Hoyt Fuller. Waukesha, Wis.: Country Beautifiul, 1976.

————. *Images of African Art Forms.* Detroit: Broadside, 1968.

————, **and Dudley Randall.** *Poem counterpoem.* Detroit: Broadside, 1969

Dent, Tom. *Blue Lights and River Songs.* Detroit: Lotus Press, 1982.

Derricotte, Toi. *Captivity.* Pittsburgh: University of Pittsburgh Press, 1989.

————. *The Empress of the Death House.* Detroit: Lotus Press, 1991.

————. *Natural Birth.* Trumansburg, N.Y.: Crossing Press, 1983.

Deveaux, Alexis. *Spirits in the Street.* Garden City, N.Y.: Doubleday, 1973.

Diggs, Alfred. *Naturally Black.* Privately printed, 1969.

Dixon, Melvin. *Change of Territory.* Lexington: University Press of Kentucky, 1983.

————. *Love's Instruments.* Chicago: Ti Chucha, 1995.

Dodson, Owen. *The Confession Stone: Song Cycles.* Heritage 13. London: Paul Bremen, 1971.

————. *Powerful Long Ladder.* New York: Farrar, 1947.

Dooley, Ebon (Thomas). *Revolution: A Poem.* Chicago: Third World Press, 1968.

Dove, Rita. *The Darker Face of the Earth: A Verse Play in Fourteen Scenes.* Brownsville, Oreg.: Storyline Press, 1994.

———. *Grace Notes.* New York: Norton, 1989.

———. *Mother Love: Poems.* New York: Norton, 1995.

———. *Museum.* Pittsburgh, Pa.: Carnegie-Mellon University Press, 1986.

———. *Selected Poems.* New York: Vintage, 1993.

———. *Thomas and Beulah.* Pittsburgh, Pa.: Carnegie-Mellon University Press, 1983.

———. *The Yellow House on the Corner.* Pittsburgh, Pa.: Carnegie-Mellon University Press, 1980.

Dumas, Henry. *Knees of a Natural Man: The Selected Poetry.* Edited with an Introduction by Eugene Redmond. New York: Thunder's Mouth, 1989.

———. *Play Ebony, Play Ivory.* New York: Random House, 1974.

Dunbar, Paul Laurence. *The Collected Poetry.* Edited with an Introduction by Joanne Braxton. Charlottesville: University Press of Virginia, 1993.

Durem, Ray. *Take No Prisoners.* Heritage 17. London: Paul Bremen, 1971.

Eckels, Jon. *Our Business in the Streets.* Detroit: Broadside, 1971.

Emanuel, James. *Panther Man.* Detroit: Broadside, 1970.

Espada, Martin. *City of Coughing and Dead Radiators.* New York: Norton, 1993.

———. *Imagine the Angels of Bread: Poems.* New York: Norton, 1996.

———. *Rebellion Is the Secret of a Lover's Hands/ Rebellion es el giro de manos del umante.* Translation into Spanish by Camilo Perez-Bustillo and the author. Willimantic, Conn.: Curbstone, 1990.

———. *Trumpets from the Islands of Their Eviction.* Tempe, Ariz.: Bilingual, 1994.

Evans, Mari. *A Dark and Splendid Mass.* New York: Harlem River, 1992.

———. *I Am a Black Woman.* New York: William Morrow, 1970.

———. *Nightstar: 1973–1978.* Los Angeles: Center for Afro-American Studies, UCLA, 1981.

Fields, Julia. *Slow Coins: New Poems and Some Old Ones.* Washington, D.C.: Three Continents, 1981.

Figueroa, Jose-Angel. *East 110th Street.* Detroit: Broadside, 1973.

Forbes, Calvin. *Blue Monday.* Wesleyan Poetry Program, 70. Hanover, N.H.: Wesleyan/University Press of New England, 1974.

Forman, Ruth. *We Are the Young Magicians.* Boston: Beacon, 1993.

Fuller, Chester. *Spend Sad Sundays Singing Songs to Sassy Sisters.* Chicago: Third World Press, 1974.

Gayles, Gloria Wade. *Anointed to Fly.* New York: Harlem River, 1991.

Gilbert, Zack. *My Own Hallelujahs.* Chicago: Third World Press, 1971.

Giovanni, Nikki. *Black Feeling, Black Talk.* Detroit: Broadside, 1968.

———. *Black Judgement.* Detroit: Broadside, 1970.

———. *Black Judgement Black Feeling Black Talk.* New York: William Morrow, 1970.

———. *Cotton Candy on a Rainy Day.* New York: William Morrow, 1980.

————. *Ego-Tripping and Other Poems for Young People.* New York: Lawrence Hill, 1973.

————. *Love Poems.* New York: William Morrow, 1997.

————. *My House.* New York: William Morrow, 1972.

————. *Re: Creation.* Detroit: Broadside, 1970.

————. *Selected Poems.* New York: William Morrow, 1996.

————. *Those Who Ride the Night Wind.* New York: William Morrow, 1983.

————. *The Women and the Men.* New York: William Morrow, 1975.

Gonsalves, Roy. *Evening Sunshine.* New York: Renaissance, 1988.

Greenlee, Sam. *Blues for an African Princess.* Chicago: Third World Press, 1971.

Hamer, Forrest. *Call and Response: Poems.* Farmington, Maine: Alice James Books, 1995.

Hammon, Jupiter. *Jupiter Hammon: American Negro Poet, Selections from His Writings and a Bibliography.* Selections by Oscar Wegelin. Miami, Fla.: Mnemosyne, 1969.

Harper, Frances Ellen Watkins. *Complete Poems.* Edited by Maryemma Graham. New York: Oxford University Press, 1988.

Harper, Michael S. *Dear John, Dear Coltrane.* Pittsburgh, Pa.: University of Pittsburgh Press, 1970.

————. *Debridement.* Garden City, N.Y.: Doubleday, 1973.

————. *Healing Song for the Inner Ear.* Urbana: University of Illinois Press, 1985.

————. *Honorable Amendments.* Urbana: University of Illinois Press, 1995.

————. *Images of Kin: New and Selected Poems.* Urbana: University of Illinois Press, 1977.

————. *Nightmare Begins Responsibility.* Urbana: University of Illinois Press, 1975.

————. *Song: I Want a Witness.* Pittsburgh, Pa.: University of Pittsburgh Press, 1972.

Hayden, Robert. *American Journal: Poems.* New York: Liveright, 1982.

————. *Angle of Ascent: New and Selected Poems.* New York: Liveright, 1975.

————. *Collected Poems.* Edited by Frederick Glaysher, with an Introduction by Arnold Rampersad. New York: Liveright-Norton, 1996.

————. *The Night-Blooming Cereus.* Heritage 20. London: Paul Bremen, 1973.

————. *Selected Poems.* New York: October House, 1970.

————. *Words in the Mourning Time.* New York: October House, 1970.

Hemphill, Essex. *Conditions.* Washington, DC: BeBop, 1986.

————. *Earth Life.* Washington, D.C.: BeBop, 1985.

Henderson, David. *De Mayor of Harlem.* New York: Dutton, 1970.

Henderson-Holmes, Safiya. *Madness and a Bit of Hope.* New York: Harlem River, 1990.

Hoaglund, Everett. *Black Velvet.* Detroit: Broadside, 1970.

Hord, Fred. *After (H)ours.* First Poets. Chicago: Third World Press, 1974.

Hughes, Langston. *Complete Poems.* Edited by Arnold Rampersad and Thomas Roessel, associate editor. New York: Knopf, 1994.

———. *Don't You Turn Back.* New York: Knopf, 1969. Poems for children selected by Lee Bennet Hopkins.

———. *The Dream Keeper.* New York: Knopf, 1932.

———. *Fields of Wonder.* New York, Knopf, 1947.

———. *Fine Clothes to the Jew.* New York: Knopf, 1927.

———. *Good Morning Revolution: Uncollected Writings of Social Protest.* Edited with an Introduction by Faith Berry. Forward by Saunders Redding. New York: Lawrence Hill, 1973.

———. *Montage of a Dream Deferred.* New York: Knopf, 1951.

———. *One-Way Ticket.* New York: Knopf, 1949.

———. *The Panther and the Lash.* New York: Knopf, 1967.

———. *Selected Poems.* New York: Knopf, 1958.

———. *Shakespeare in Harlem.* New York: Knopf, 1942.

———. *The Weary Blues.* New York: Knopf, 1926.

Hull, Gloria T. *Healing Heart: Poems 1973–1988.* Albany, N.Y.: Kitchen Table, 1989.

Jackson, Angela. *Dark Legs and Silk Kisses: The Beatitudes of the Spinners.* Evanston, Ill.: Northwestern University Press, 1993.

———. *Solo in the Box Car Third Floor E.* Chicago: OBAhouse, 1985.

———. *Voo Doo/ Love Magic.* Chicago: Third World Press, 1974.

Jackson, Mae. *Can I Poet with You.* Detroit: Broadside, 1969.

Jeffers, Lance. *Grandsire.* Detroit: Lotus Press, 1979.

———. *My Blackness Is the Beauty of This Land.* Detroit: Broadside, 1970.

———. *O Africa Where I Baked My Bread.* Detroit: Lotus Press, 1977.

———. *When I Know the Power of My Black Hand.* Detroit: Broadside, 1974.

Joans, Ted. *Afrodisia.* New York: Hill and Wang, 1970.

———. *Black Pow Wow.* New York: Hill and Wang, 1969.

———. *Mehr Blitzliebe Poems.* A bilingual edition. Hamburg: Verlag Michael Kellner, 1982.

Johnson, James Weldon. *God's Trombones: Seven Negro Sermons in Verse.* 1927. New York: Viking Compass, 1969.

———. *St. Peter Relates an Incident and Other Poems.* New York: Penguin, 1993.

Jones, Gayl. *The Hermit Woman.* Detroit: Lotus Press, 1981.

———. *Song for Anninho.* Detroit: Lotus Press, 1981.

———. *Xarque and Other Poems.* Detroit: Lotus Press, 1985.

Jones, LeRoi. See Baraka, Amiri.

Jones, Patricia Spears. *The Weather That Kills.* Minneapolis, Minn.: Coffee House Press, 1995.

Jordan, June. *Haruko/ Love Poems: New and Selected Love Poems.* New York: High Risk, 1994.

———. *Naming Our Destiny: New and Selected Poems.* New York: Thunder's Mouth, 1989.

————. *New Days: Poems of Exile and Return.* New York: Emerson Hall, 1974.

————. *Passion: New Poems, 1977–1980.* Boston: Beacon, 1980.

————. *Some Changes.* Black Poets Series. New York: Dutton, 1971.

————. *Things that I Do in the Dark: Selected Poems.* New York: Random House, 1977.

Jordan, Norman. *Destination: Ashes.* Chicago: Third World, 1970.

Kaufman, Bob. *Cranial Guitar: Selected Poems.* Edited by Gerald Nicosia. Minneapolis: Coffee House Press, 1996.

————. *Golden Sardine.* San Francisco: City Lights, 1967.

————. *Solitudes Crowded with Loneliness.* New York: New Directions, 1965.

Kendrick, Dolores. *Now Is the Thing to Praise.* Detroit: Lotus Press, 1984.

————. *Through the Ceiling.* Heritage 24. London: Paul Bremen, 1975.

————. *The Women of Plums: Poems in the Voices of Slave Women.* New York: William Morrow, 1989.

Knight, Etheridge. *Belly Song and Other Poems.* Detroit: Broadside, 1973.

————. *Born of a Woman: New and Selected Poems.* Boston: Houghton, 1980.

————. *The Essential Etheridge Knight.* Pittsburgh, Pa.: University of Pittsburgh Press, 1986.

————. *Poems from Prison.* Detroit: Broadside, 1969,

Komunyakaa, Yusef. *Copasetic.* Middletown, Conn.: Wesleyan University Press, 1984.

————. *Dien Cai Dau.* Middletown, Conn.: Wesleyan University Press, 1988.

————. *I Apologize for the Eyes in My Head.* Middletown, Conn.: Wesleyan University Press, 1986.

————. *Lost in the Bonewheel Factory: Poems.* Lynx House, 1971.

————. *Magic City.* Hanover N.H.: University Press of New England, 1992.

————. *Neon Vernacular: New and Selected Poems.* Hanover, N.H.: Wesleyan/University Press of New England, 1993.

The Last Poets. *On a Mission: Selected Poems and a History.* By Abiodun Oyewole and Umar Bin Hassan with Kim Green. Forward by Amiri Baraka. New York: Owl-Holt, 1996.

Lee, Don L. See Madhubuti, Haki R.

Lomax, Pearl Cleage. *We Don't Need No Music.* Detroit: Broadside, 1972.

Long, Doughtry. *Song for Nia: A Poetic Essay in Three Parts.* Detroit: Broadside, 1971.

Long, Richard A. *Ascending and Other Poems.* Privately printed, 1975.

Lorde, Audre. *The Black Unicorn.* New York: Norton, 1978.

————. *Cables to Rage.* Heritage 9. London: Paul Bremen, 1970.

————. *Chosen Poems—Old and New.* New York: Norton, 1982.

————. *Coal.* New York: Norton, 1976.

————. *From a Land Where Other People Live.* Detroit: Broadside, 1973.

————. *The Marvelous Arithmetics of Distance: Poems 1987–1992.* New York: Norton, 1993.

————. *The New York Head Shop and Museum.* Detroit: Broadside, 1974.

————. *Our Dead Behind Us.* New York: Norton, 1986.

————. *Undersong: Chosen Poems Old and New, Revised.* New York: Norton, 1992.

Madgett, Naomi Long. *Octavia and Other Poems.* Chicago: Third World Press, 1988.

Madhubuti, Haki R. (Don L. Lee). *Book of Life.* Detroit: Broadside, 1973.

————. *Directionscore: Selected and New Poems.* Detroit: Broadside, 1971.

————. *Don't Cry, Scream!* Detroit: Broadside, 1969.

————. *Earthquakes amd Sun Rise Missions.* Chicago: Third World Press, 1983.

————. *HeartLove: Wedding and Love Poems.* Chicago: ThirdWorld, 1998.

————. *Killing Memory, Seeking Ancestors.* Detroit: Lotus Press, 1987.

————. *Think Black.* Detroit: Broadside, 1967.

————. *We Walk the Way of the New World.* Detroit: Broadside, 1970.

Maga (Jackson). *Poems/ Words for My Black Brothers and Sisters.* Privately printed, 1969.

Mahone, Barbara. *Sugarfields.* Detroit: Broadside, 1970.

Major, Clarence. *The Cotton Club.* Detroit: Broadside, 1972.

————. *Symptons and Madness.* New York: Corinth, 1971.

Mataka, Laini (Wanda Robinson). *Never as Strangers.* Baltimore: Du Forcelf/ Black Classic, 1988.

McKay, Claude. *Selected Poems.* With a biographical note by Max Eastman. New York: Harvest, 1943.

Miller, E. Ethelbert. *Migrant Worker.* Washington, D.C.: Writers, 1978.

————. *Season of Hunger/ Cry of Rain.* Detroit: Lotus Press, 1982.

————. *Where Are the Love Poems for Dictators.* Washington, D.C.: Open Hand, 1986.

Mor, (David) Amus. *The Coming of John.* Privately printed, 1969.

Moss, Thylias. *Small Congregations: New and Selected Poems.* Hopewell, N.J.: Ecco Press, 1993.

Muhajir, El (Marvin X). *Black Man Listen.* Detroit: Broadside, 1969.

————. *Woman–Man's Best Friend: Parables Proverbs Poems Songs.* San Francisco: Al Kitab Sudan, 1973.

Murphy, Beatrice M., and Nancy L. Arnez. *The Rocks Cry Out.* Detroit: Broadside, 1969.

Murray, Pauli. *Dark Testament and Other Poems.* New York: Silvermine, 1970.

Neal, Larry. *Black Boogaloo: Notes on Black Liberation.* San Francisco: Jrl Black Poetry, 1969.

————. *HooDoo Hollerin' BeBop Ghosts.* Washington, D.C.: Howard University Press, 1974.

————. *Visions of a Liberated Future: Black Arts Movement Writings.* With commentary by Amiri Baraka, Stanley Crouch, Charles Fuller, and Jayne Cortez. Edited by Michael Schwartz. New York: Thunder's Mouth, 1989.

Nelson (Waniek), Marilyn. *The Fields of Praise: New and Selected Poems.* Baton Rouge: Louisiana State University Press, 1997.

————. *The Homeplace.* Baton Rouge: Louisiana State University Press, 1990.

————. *Magnificat.* Baton Rouge: Louisiana State University Press, 1994.

————. *Partial Truth.* Baton Rouge: Louisiana State University Press, 1992.

Nichols, Marion. *Life Styles.* Detroit: Broadside: 1971.

Olumo (jim cunningham). *The Blue Narrator.* First Poets. Chicago: Third World, 1974.

Osbey, Brenda Marie. *Ceremony for Minnieconjoux.* Lexington: University of Kentucky Press, 1983.

————. *In These Houses.* Hanover, N.H.: Wesleyan/University Press of New England, 1988.

Parker, Pat. *Child of Myself.* Oakland, Calif.: Women's Press Collective, 1974.

————. *Jonestown and Other Madness.* Ithaca, N.Y.: Firebrand, 1985.

————. *Movement in Black: Collected Poetry.* Oakland, Calif.: Diana, 1978.

————. *Pit Stop.* Oakland, Calif.: Women's Press Collective, 1975.

Patterson, Raymond. *26 Ways of Looking at a Black Man.* New York: Award, 1969.

Perkins, Eugene. See Useni.

Pietri, Pedro. *Puerto Rican Obituary.* New York: Monthly Review, 1973.

Plumpp, Sterling D. *Blues: The Story Always Untold.* Chicago: Another Chicago Press, 1989.

————. *Half Black Half Blacker.* Chicago: Third World Press, 1970.

————. *The Mojo Hands Call, I Must Go.* New York: Thunder's Mouth, 1982.

————. *Portable Soul.* Chicago: Third World Press, 1969.

————. *Steps to Break the Circle.* Chicago: Third World Press, 1974.

Ra, Jamilla (Maxine Hall Ellison). *The Good Book.* Chicago: Jamaa Scenes, 1971.

Randall, Dudley. *After the Killing.* Chicago: Third World Press, 1973.

————. *Cities and Other Disasters.* Detroit: Broadside, 1973.

————. *Cities Burning.* Detroit: Broadside, 1968.

————. *A Litany of Friends: New and Selected Poems.* Detroit: Lotus Press, 1981.

————. *Love You.* Heritage 10. London: Paul Bremen, 1970.

————. *More to Remember.* Chicago: Third World Press, 1971.

————, **and Margaret Danner.** *Poem Counterpoem.* Detroit: Broadside, 1969.

Raven, John. *Blues for Momma and Other Low Down Stuff.* Detroit, Mich: Broadside, 1971.

Reddy, T.J. *Less than a Score but a Point.* New York: Vintage, 1971.

Redmond, Eugene B. *Sentry of the Four Golden Pillars.* Privately printed, 1970.

Songs from an Afro/ Phone: New Poems. East St. Louis, Ill.: Black River Writers, 1972.

Reed, Ishmael. *Cab Calloway Stands in for the Moon.* Flint, Mich.: Bamberger, 1970.

——. *Catechism of d Neoamerican Hoodoo Church.* Heritage 11. London: Paul Bremen, 1970.

——. *Chattanooga.* New York: Random House, 1973.

——. *Conjure.* Amherst: University of Massachusetts Press, 1972.

——. *New and Selected Poems.* New York: Atheneum, 1988.

——. *A Secretary to the Spirits.* Illustrated by Betye Saar. New York: NOK, 1978.

Rivers, Conrad Kent. *The Still Voice of Harlem.* Heritage 5. London: Paul Bremen, 1972.

——. *The Wright Poems.* Introduced by Ronald Fair. Heritage 18. London: Paul Bremen, 1972.

Rodgers, Carolyn. *The Heart as Ever Green: New and Selected Poems.* New York: Doubleday, 1978.

——. *How I Got Ovah: New and Selected Poems.* New York: Doubleday, 1975.

——. *Paper Soul.* Chicago: Third World Press, 1968.

——. *Songs of a Black Bird.* Chicago: Third World Press, 1969.

——. *Two Love Raps.* Chicago: Third World Press, 1969.

Roland, Larry. *As Time Flows On.* Privately printed, 1977.

Royster, Philip M. *The Back Door.* Chicago: Third World Press, 1971.

——. *Songs and Dances: Selected Poems.* Detroit: Lotus Press, 1981.

Royster, Sandra. *Women Talk.* First Poets. Chicago: Third World Press, 1974.

Rushin, Kate. *The Black Back-Ups.* Ithaca, N.Y.:Firebrand, 1993.

Ya Salaam, Kalamu (val ferdinand). *Hofi Ni Kwenu–My Fear Is For You.* New Orleans, La.: Ahidiana, 1973. Essays and poetry.

——. *Pamoja Tutashinda Together We Will Win.* New Orleans, La.: Ahidiana, 1974.

Sanchez, Sonia. *Blues Book for Blue Black Magical Women.* Detroit: Broadside, 1971.

——. *Does Your House Have Lions?* Boston: Beacon Press, 1997.

——. *Homecoming.* Detroit: Broadside, 1969.

——. *Homegirls and Handgrenades.* New York: Thunder's Mouth, 1984.

——. *It's A New Day.* Detroit: Broadside, 1971. Children's poems.

——. *I've Been a Woman: New and Selected Poems.* Sausalito, Calif.: Black Scholar, 1978.

——. *Like the Singing Coming Off the Drums: Love Poems.* Boston: Beacon Press, 1998.

——. *Under a Soprano Sky.* Trenton, N.J.: Africa World, 1997.

——. *We A Baddd People.* Detroit: Broadside, 1970.

——. *Wounded in the House of a Friend.* Boston: Beacon, 1995.

Scott-Heron, Gil. *Small Talk at 125th and Lenox.* New York: World, 1970.

——. *So Far, So Good.* Chicago: Third World Press, 1990.

Shange, Ntozake. *For Colored Girls Who Have Considered Suicide when the Rainbow Is Enuf: A Choreopoem.* New York: Macmillan, 1977.

——. *A Daughter's Geography.* New York: St. Martin's, 1983.

————. *The Love Space Demands (A Continuing Saga)*. New York: St. Martin's, 1991.

————. *Nappy Edges*. New York: St Martin's, 1978.

————. *Ridin' the Moon in Texas: Word Paintings*. New York: St. Martin's, 1987.

————. *See No Evil: Prefaces, Essays and Accounts 1976–1983*. San Francisco: Momo's, 1984.

Simmons, Judy Dothard. *Judith's Blues*. Detroit: Broadside, 1973.

Smith, Patricia. *Big Towns, Big Talk*. Cambridge, Mass.: Zoland Books, 1992.

————. *Close to Death*. Cambridge, Mass.: Zoland Books, 1993.

————. *Life According to Motown*. Chicago: Tia Chucha, 1991.

Snellings, Roland. See Toure, Askia Muhammad.

Stephany. *Moving Deep*. Detroit: Broadside, 1969.

Thigpen, William A. *Down Nigger Paved Streets*. Detroit: Broadside, 1972.

Thomas, Lorenzo. *The Bathers*. Berkeley, Calif.: I. Reed, 1981.

Tolson, Melvin B. *A Gallery of Harlem Portraits*. 1935. Edited with an afterword by Robert M. Farnsworth. Columbia: University of Missouri Press, 1979.

————. *Harlem Gallery*. New York: Twayne, 1965,

————. *Libretto for the Republic of Liberia*. Preface by Allen Tate. African American Library. New York: Twayne, 1963.

Toure, Askia Muhammad (Roland Snellings). *From the Pyramids to the Projects: Poems of Genocide and Resistance*. Trenton, N.J.: Africa World, 1990.

————. *Juju (Magic Songs for the Black Nation)*. Chicago: Third World Press, 1970.

————. *Songhai!* New York: Songhai, 1972.

Troupe, Quincy. *Weather Reports: New and Selected Poems*. New York: Harlem River, 1991.

Useni (Eugene Perkins). *An Apology to My African Brother*. Chicago: Free Black, 1995.

————. *Black Is Beautiful*. Chicago: Free Black, 1968.

————. *Midnight Blues in the Afternoon and Other Poems*. Chicago: INESU, 1984.

————. *Silhouette*. Chicago: Free Black, 1970.

————. *When You Grow Up and Other Children's Poems*. Chicago: Free Black, 1977.

Vest, Hilda. *Sorrow's End*. Detroit: Broadside, 1993.

Walker, Alice. *Good Night, Willie Lee, I'll See You in the Morning*. New York: Dial, 1979.

————. *Her Blue Body Everything We Know: Earthling Poems 1965–1990. Complete Poems*. San Diego, Calif.: Harvest-Harcourt, 1991.

————. *Horses Make a Landscape Look More Beautiful*. San Diego, Calif.: Harcourt, 1984.

————. *Once.* New York: Harcourt, 1970.

————. *Revolutionary Petunias.* New York: Harcourt, 1972.

Walker, Margaret. *For My People and Other Poems.* New Haven, Conn.: Yale University Press, 1942.

————. *October Journey.* Detroit: Broadside, 1973.

————. *Prophets for a New Day.* Detroit: Broadside, 1970.

————. *This Is My Century: New and Collected Poems.* Athens: University of Georgia Press, 1989.

Waniek, Marilyn Nelson. See Nelson, Marilyn.

Warr, Michael. *We Are All the Black Boy.* Chicago: Tia Chucha, 1991.

Weatherly, Tom. *Maumau American Cantos.* New York: Corinth, 1970.

Weaver, Michael S. *Timber and Prayer: The Indian Pond Poems.* Pittsburgh, Pa.: University of Pittsburgh Press, 1995.

————. *Water Song.* Lexington: University Press of Kentucky, 1985.

Wheatley, Phillis. *The Poems (1767–1784).* Rev. and enl. ed. Edited with an introduction by Julian D. Mason, Jr. Chapel Hill: University of North Carolina Press, 1989.

Williams, Jeannette. *Sapphire.* Chicago: Free Black, 1970.

Williams, Sherley Ann. *The Peacock Poems.* Middletown, Conn.: Wesleyan University Press, 1975.

————. *Some One Sweet Angel Chile.* New York: William Morrow, 1982.

Wimberli, Sigemonde. *Ghetto Scenes.* Chicago: Free Black, 1968.

Wolde, Habte. *Enough to Die For.* Chicago: Free Black, 1972.

Wright, Jay. *Dimensions of History.* Santa Cruz, Calif.: Kayak Books, 1976.

Wright, Jay. *The Double Invention of Komo.* Austin: University of Texas Press, 1980.

————. *Explications/ Interpretations.* Lexington: University Press of Kentucky, 1984.

————. *The Homecoming Singer.* New York: Corinth, 1971.

————. *Selected Poems.* Edited with an introduction by Robert B. Stepto. Afterword by Harold Bloom. Princeton, N.J.: Princeton University Press, 1987.

————. *Soothsayers and Omens.* Seven Woods, 1976.

Young, Al. *The Blues Don't Change: New and Selected Poems.* Baton Rouge: Louisiana State University Press, 1982.

————. *Geography of the Near Past.* New York: Holt, 1976.

————. *The Song Turning Back into Itself.* New York: Holt, 1971.

Young, Kevin. *Most Way Home.* New York: William Morrow, 1995.

Zubena, Sister (Cynthia Conley). *Calling All Sisters.* Chicago: Free Black, 1969.

————. *Om Black.* Chicago: Free Black, 1970.

Zu-Bolton, Ahmos. *Ain't No Spring Chicken: Selected Poetry and Folklore.* New Orleans, La.: Louisiana Foundation of Folklore and Storytelling/ Copasetic, 1991.

CRITICISM, BOOKS

Abrahams, Roger D. *Deep Down in the Jungle: Negro Narrative Folklore from the Streets of Philadelphia.* Chicago: Aldine, 1970.

————. *Singing the Master: The Emergence of African-American Culture in the Plantation South.* New York: Penguin, 1992.

————, **and Abraham Szwed,** eds. *After Africa.* New Haven, Conn.: Yale University Press, 1983.

Asante, Molefi Kete. *African and African American Communication Continuities.* Council on International Studies: Special Studies #61. Buffalo: State University of New York, 1975.

————. *The Afrocentric Idea.* Philadelphia: Temple University Press, 1987.

Baker, Houston A., Jr. *Black Studies, Rap and the Academy.* Chicago: University of Chicago Press, 1993.

————. *Blues, Ideology, and Afro-American Literature: A Vernacular Theory.* Chicago: University of Chicago Press, 1984.

————. *A Many-Colored Coat of Dreams: The Poetry of Countee Cullen.* Broadside Critics 4. Detroit: Broadside, 1974.

————. *Modernism and the Harlem Renaissance.* Chicago: University of Chicago Press, 1987.

————, **and Patricia Redmond,** eds. *Afro-American Literary Study in the 1990s.* Chicago: University of Chicago Press, 1989.

Baraka, Amiri. *The Autobiography of LeRoi Jones/ Amiri Baraka.* New York: Freundlich, 1984.

————. *Black Music.* New York: Quill, 1967.

Barlow, William. *Looking Up at Down: The Emergence of Blues Culture*: Philadelphia: Temple University Press, 1989.

Bell, Bernard W. *The Folk Roots of Contemporary Afro-American Poetry.* Broadside Critics 3. Detroit: Broadside, 1974.

Bellamy, Joe David, ed. *American Poetry Observed: Poets on Their Work.* Urbana: University of Illinois Press, 1984.

Bentson, Kimberly W., ed. *Imamu Amiri Baraka (LeRoi Jones): A Collection of Critical Essays.* Englewood Cliffs, N.J.: Prentice-Hall, 1978.

Bercovitch, Sacvan, ed. *Reconstructing American Literary History.* Harvard English Studies 13. Cambridge: Harvard University Press, 1986.

Berube, Michael. *Marginal Forces/ Cultural Centers: Tolson, Pynchon and the Politics of the Canon.* Ithaca, N.Y.: Cornell University Press, 1992.

Brooks, Gwendolyn. *Report from Part One.* Detroit: Broadside, 1972.

————. *Report from Part Two.* Chicago: Third World Press, 1996.

Butcher, Phillip, ed. *The William Statley Braithwaite Reader.* Ann Arbor: University of Michigan Press, 1972.

Cartey, Wilfred G. *Black Images.* New York: Teachers College, 1970.

Cook, Mercer, and Stephen Henderson. *The Militant Black Writer.* Madison: University of Wisconsin Press, 1969.

Dance, Daryl Cumber. *Shuckin' and Jivin': Folklore from Contemporary Black Americans.* Bloomington: University of Indiana Press, 1978.

Davis, Angela Y. *Blues Legacies and Black Feminism: Gertrude "Ma" Rainey, Bessie Smith, and Billie Holiday.* New York: Pantheon, 1998.

Dillard, J. L. *Black English: Its History and Usage in the United States.* New York: Vintage, 1973.

Doreski, William. *The Modern Voice in American Poetry.* Miami: University of Florida Press, 1995.

Dunbar-Nelson, Alice. *Give Us Each Day: The Diary.* Edited with a critical introduction and notes by Gloria T. Hull. New York: Norton, 1984.

Dundes, Alan, ed. *Mother Wit from the Laughing Barrel: Readings in the Interpretation of Afro-American Folklore.* Jackson: University Press of Mississippi, 1990.

Fernando, S. H., Jr. *The New Beats: Exploring the Music, Culture, and Attitudes Of Hip-Hop.* New York: Doubleday-Anchor, 1994.

Finnegan, Ruth. *Oral Poetry: Its Nature, Significance and Social Context.* London: Cambridge University Press, 1977.

Fisher, Dexter, and Robert B. Stepto, eds. *Afro-American Literature: The Reconstruction of Instruction.* New York: MLA, 1979.

Fowler, Virgina C., ed. *Conversations with Nikki Giovanni.* Jackson: University Press of Mississippi, 1992.

Gabbin, Joanne V. *Sterling A. Brown: Building the Black Aesthetic Tradition.* Charlottesville: University Press of Virginia, 1985.

Gates, Henry Louis, Jr., *The Signifying Monkey: A Theory of African-American Literary Criticism.* New York: Oxford University Press, 1988.

Gayle, Addison, Jr., ed. *The Black Aesthetic.* New York: Doubleday, 1971.

———.*Black Expressions: Essays by and about Black Americans in the Creative Arts.* New York: Weybright and Talley, 1969.

George, Nelson. *Buppies, B-Boys, Baps and Bohos: Notes on Post-Soul Black Culture.* New York: HarperCollins, 1992.

Gibson, Donald B., ed. *Modern Black Poets: A Collection of Critical Essays.* Englewood Cliffs, N.J.: Prentice-Hall, 1973.

Gilbert, Sandra M., and Susan Gubar, eds. *Shakespeare's Sisters: Feminist Essays on Women Poets.* Bloomington: Indiana University Press, 1979.

Gilroy, Paul. *The Black Atlantic: Modernity and Double Consciousness.* Cambridge: Harvard University Press, 1993.

Harris, Marie, and Kathleen Aguero, eds. *A Gift of Tongues: Critical Challenges In Contemporary American Poetry.* Athens: University of Georgia Press, 1987.

Haslam, Geral W. *Afro-American Oral Literature.* New York: Harper and Row, 1975.

Hatcher, John. *From the Auroral Darkness: The Life and Poetry of Robert Hayden.* New York: Oxford University Press, 1984.

Hoffman, Daniel, ed. *Harvard Guide to Contemporary American Writing.* Cambridge: Harvard University Press, 1979.

Hogue, W. Lawrence. *Discourse and the Other: The Production of the Afro-American Text.* Durham, N.C.: Duke University Press, 1986.

———. *Race, Modernity, Postmodernity: A Look at the History and Literature of Literatures of People of Color since the 1960s.* Albany: State University of New York Press, 1996.

Howard-Pitney, David. *The Afro-American Jeremiad: Appeals for Justice in America.* Philadelphia: Temple University Press, 1990.

Hubbard, Dolan. *The Sermon and the African American Literary Imagination.* Columbus: University of Missouri Press, 1994.

Hudson, Theodore R. *From LeRoi Jones to Amiri Baraka: The Literary Works.* Durham, N.C.: Duke University Press, 1973.

Huggins, Nathan Irvin. *Harlem Renaissance.* New York: Oxford University Press, 1971.

Jackson, Bruce, ed. *"Get Your Ass in the Water and Swim Like Me": Narrative Poetry from Black Oral Tradition.* Cambridge: Harvard University Press, 1974.

———. *Wake Up Dead Man: Afro-American Worksongs from Texas.* Cambridge: Harvard University Press, 1972.

Jahn, Janheinz. *Muntu: An Outline of the New African Culture.* New York: Grove, 1961.

Johnson, Clifton H., and Paul Radin, eds. *God Struck Me Dead: Religious Conversion Experiences and Autobiographies of Ex-Slaves.* Philadelphia: Pilgrim, 1969.

Jones, Gayl. *Liberating Voices: Oral Tradition in African American Literature.* New York: Penguin, 1991.

Joyce, Joyce Ann. *IjaLa.: Sonia Sanchez and the African Poetic Tradition.* Chicago: Third World Press, 1996.

———. *Warriors, Conjurers and Priests: Defining African-Centered Literary Criticism.* Chicago: Third World Press, 1994.

Jordan, June. *On Call: Political Essays.* Boston: South End, 1985.

Katz, Bernard, ed. *The Social Implications of Early Negro Music in the United States.* New York: Arno, 1969. Reprints of essays written 1862–1939.

Kent, George. *Blackness and the Adventure of Western Culture.* Chicago: Third World Press, 1973.

———. *A Life of Gwendolyn Brooks.* Lexington: University Press of Kentucky, 1990.

King, Woodie, and Earl Anthony, eds. *Black Poets and Prophets: The Theory, Practice and Esthetics of the Pan-Africanist Revolution.* New York: New American Library, 1972.

Kochman, Thomas, ed. *Rappin' and Stylin' Out: Communication in Urban Black America.* Urbana: University of Illinois Press, 1972.

Krehbiel, Henry Edward. *Afro-American Folksongs: A Study in Racial and National Music.* 1913. Reprint, New York: Ungar, 1962.

Lee, Don L. *Dynamite Voices: Black Poets of the 1960's.* Broadside Critics 1. Detroit: Broadside, 1971.

Levine, Lawrence W. *Black Culture and Black Consciousness: Afro-American Folk Thought from Slavery to Freedom.* New York: Oxford University Press, 1977.

Levy, Eugene. *James Weldon Johnson: Black Leader, Black Voice.* Chicago: University of Chicago Press, 1973.

Lord, Albert B. *The Singer of Tales.* Cambridge: Harvard University Press, 1960.

Major, Clarence. *The Dark and Feeling: Black American Writers and Their Work.* New York: Third Press, 1974.

———. *Juba to Jive: A Dictionary of African-American Slang.* New York: Penguin, 1994.

Melheim, D. H. *Gwendolyn Brooks: Poetry and the Heroic Voice.* Lexington: University Press of Kentucky, 1987.

———. *Heroism in the New Black Poetry: Introductions and Interviews.* Lexington: University Press of Kentucky, 1990.

Miller, R. Baxter, ed. *Black American Poets Between Worlds. 1940–1960.* Knoxville: University of Tennessee Press, 1986.

Mootry, Maria K., and Gary Smith, eds. *A Life Distilled: Gwendolyn Brooks, Her Poetry and Fiction.* Urbana: University of Illinois Press, 1989.

Murray, Albert. *The Blue Devils of Nada: A Contemporary American Approach to Aesthetic Statement.* New York: Pantheon, 1996.

———. *The Omni-Americans: New Perspectives on Black Experience and American Culture.* New York: Discus, 1970.

———. *Stomping the Blues.* New York: McGraw-Hill, 1976.

Nelson, Havelock, and Michael A. Gonzalez. *Bring the Noise: A Guide to Rap Music and Hip Hop Culture.* New York: Harmony, 1991.

Nielsen, Aldon Lynn. *Black Chant: Languages of African-American Postmodernism.* Cambridge: Cambridge University Press, 1997.

O'Brien, John. *Interviews with Black Writers.* New York: Liveright, 1973.

O'Daniel, Therman B., ed. *Langston Hughes, Black Genius: A Critical Evaluation.* New York: William Morrow, 1971.

Ong, Walter J. *Orality and Literacy: The Technologizing of the Word.* London: Routledge, 1982.

Rampersad, Arnold. *The Life of Langston Hughes.* Vol. I: *1902–1941, I Too, Sing America.* New York: Oxford University Press, 1986.

———. *The Life of Langston Hughes.* Vol. II: *1942–1965, I Dream a World.* New York: Oxford University Press, 1988.

Redmond, Eugene B. *Drumvoices: The Mission of Afro-American Poetry.* New York: Anchor-Doubleday, 1976.

Reilly, Charles, ed. *Conversations with Amiri Baraka.* Jackson: University Press of Mississippi, 1994.

Robinson, William H. *Phillis Wheatley in the Black American Beginnings.* Broadside Critics 5. Detroit: Broadside Press, 1975.

Roscoe, Adrian A. *Mother Is Gold: A Study in West African Literature.* Cambridge, Mass.: Cambridge University Press, 1971.

Rose, Tricia. *Black Noise: Rap Music and Black Culture in Contemporary America.* Hanover, N.H.: Wesleyan/University Press of New England, 1994.

Rosenberg, Bruce A. *The Art of the American Folk Preacher.* New York: Oxford University Press, 1970.

Schipper, Mineke. *Beyond the Boundaries: African Literature and Literary Theory.* London: Allison and Busby, 1989.

Sexton, Adam, ed. *Rap on Rap: Straight-up Talk on Hip-Hop Culture.* New York: Delta, 1995.

Smitherman, Geneva. *Black Language and Culture: Sounds of Soul.* New York: Harper and Row, 1975.

————. *Black Talk: Words and Phrases from the Hood to the Amen Corner.* Boston: Houghton Mifflin, 1994.

Sollors, Werner, and Maria Diedrich, eds. *The Black Columbiad: Defining Moments in African American Literature and Culture.* Cambridge: Harvard University Press, 1994.

Stewart, Garrett. *Reading Voices: Literature and the Phonotext.* Berkeley: University of California Press, 1990.

Stoller, Paul, ed. *Black American English: Its Background and Its Usage in the Schools and in Literature.* New York: Delta, 1975.

Tate, Greg. *Flyboy in the Buttermilk: Essays on Contemporary America.* New York: Simon and Schuster, 1992.

Todd, Loreto. *Modern Englishes: Pidgins and Creoles.* London: Blackwell, 1984.

Turco, Lewis Putnam. *Visions and Revisions of American Poetry.* Little Rock: University of Arkansas Press, 1986.

Vendler, Helen. *"The Music of What Happens": Poems, Poets, Critics.* Cambridge: Harvard University Press, 1988.

————. *Soul Says: On Recent Poetry.* Cambridge: Harvard University Press, 1995.

Wagner, Jean. *Black Poets of the United States: From Paul Laurence Dunbar to Langston Hughes.* Translated by Kenneth Douglas. Urbana: University of Illinois Press, 1973.

Williams, Pontheola T. *Robert Hayden: A Critical Analysis of His Poetry.* With an Introduction by Blyden Jackson. Urbana: University of Illinois Press, 1987.

CRITICISM, ARTICLES AND ESSAYS

Abrahams, Roger D. "Joking: The Training of the Man of Words in Talking Broad," in Kochman, *Rappin',* 215–240.

Allen, Samuel W. "Sterling Brown: Poems to Endure." *Massachusetts Review* 24 (autumn 1983): 649–657.

Bentson, Kimberly W. "Performing Blackness: Re/Placing Afro-American Poetry," in Baker and Redmond, *Afro-American Literary Study,* with responses by Cheryl A. Wall and Stephen B. Henderson, 164–193.

Blount, Marcellus. "The Preacherly Text: African American Poetry and Vernacular Performance." *PMLA* 107 (1992): 582–593.

Brown, Claude. "The Language of Soul," in Kochman, *Rappin'*, 136–139.

Brown, Fahamisha Patricia. "Rethinking the Afro-American Genre Course," in Fisher and Stepto, *Afro-American Literature*, 244–249.

Brown, H. Rap. "Street Talk," in Kochman, *Rappin'*, 205–208.

Brown, Sterling A. "The Negro in American Poetry." *Negro Poetry and Drama*, 1937. Repr. New York: Atheneum, 1969. 4–102.

Buckner, B. Dilla. "Folkloric Elements in Margaret Walker's Poems." *CLA Journal* 33 (1990): 367–377.

Calt, Stephen. "The Country Blues as Meaning." In Grossman, Grossman, and Calt, *Country Blues Songbook*, 8–35.

Dickson, L. L. "Keep it in the Head: Jazz Elements in Modern Black American Poetry." *MELUS* 19 (spring 1983).

Dumon, Maria. "Unmeaning Jargon/ Uncanonized Beatitude: Bob Kaufman Poet." *South Atlantic Quarterly* 87 (1988): 701–741.

Gates, Henry Louis, Jr. "Dis and Dat: Dialect and Descent," in Fisher and Stepto, *Afro-American Literature*, 88–119.

Harper, Michael. *"Don't They Speak Jazz."* MELUS 10 (spring 1983): 3–6.

Henderson, Stephen B. "The Forms of Things Unknown," in Henderson, *Understanding the New Black Poetry*, 3–69.

Holt, Grace Sims. "Stylin' outta the black pulpit," in Kochman, *Rappin'*, 189–204.

Horvath, Brooke Kenton. "The Satisfaction of What's Difficult in Gwendolyn Brooks's Poetry." *American Literature* 62 (1990): 606–616.

Jarab, Josef. "Black Stars, the Red Star and the Blues," in Sollors and Diedrich, *The Black Columbiad*, 167–173.

Johnson, James Weldon. "On the Negro's Creative Genius," in Johnson, *The Book of American Negro Poetry*, 3–48.

———. "Preface," in Johnson, *God's Trombones*, 1–11.

Jordan, June. "The Difficult Miracle of Black Poetry in America or Something Like a Sonnet for Phillis Wheatley," in Jordan, *On Call: Political Essays*, 87–98.

———. "For the Sake of a People's Poetry: Walt Whitman and the Rest of Us," in Jordan, *On Call: Political Essays*, 5–15.

———. "Introduction," in Jordan, *Soulscript*, xvi–xix.

Kellman, Anthony. "Projective Verse as a Mode of Socio-Linguistic Protest." *Ariel* 21 (April 1990): 45–57.

Kochman, Thomas. "Toward an Ethnography of Black American Speech Behavior," in Kochman, *Rappin'*, 241–264.

Labov, William, Paul Cohen, Clarence Robins, and John Lewis. "Toasts," in Dundes, *Mother Wit*, 329–347.

Lee, A. Robert. "'Ask Your Mama': Langston Hughes, the Blues and Recent Afro-American Literary Studies." *Journal of American Studies* 24 (1990): 199–209.

Lentz, Gunter H. "Black Poetry and Black Music, History and Tradition: Michael Harper and John Coltrane," in *History and Tradition in Afro-American Culture,* edited by Gunter H. Lentz. Frankfurt: Campus Verlag, 1984. 277–326.

Lerner, Laurence. "Poetry as the Play of Signifiers." *Essays in Criticism* 35 (1985): 238–259.

Martin, Reginald. "The New Black Aesthetic Critics and Their Exclusion from American 'Mainstream' Criticism." *College English* 50, no. 4 (April 1988): 373–382.

Melnick, Mimi Clar. "I Can Peep through Muddy Water and Spy Dry Land: Boasts in the Blues," Dundes, *Mother Wit,* 267–276.

Mitchell-Kernan, Claudia. "Signifying, Loud-talking and Marking," in Kochman, *Rappin',* 315–335.

Mootry, Maria K. "Chocolate Mabbie and Pearl May Lee: Gwendolyn Brooks and the Ballad Tradition." *CLA Journal* 30 (1987): 278–293.

Okpewho, Isidore. "The Cousins of Uncle Remus," in Sollors and Diedrich, *The Black Columbiad,* 15–27.

———. "The Nature of African Oral Poetry," in *The Heritage of African Poetry: An Anthology of Oral and Written Poetry.* Harlow, U.K.: Longman, 1985. 3–34.

Oliver, Paul. "Can't Even Write: The Blues and Ethnic Literature." *MELUS* 10 (spring 1983): 3–14.

Peters, Erskine. "The Poetics of the Afro-American Spiritual." *BALF* 23 (1989): 559–578.

Pitts, Walter. "West Africa Poetics in the Black Preaching Style." *American Speech* 64 (1989): 137–149.

Ribeo, Ugo. "Voice as Lifesaver: Defining the Function of Orality in Etheridge Knight's Poetry," in Sollors and Diedrich, *The Black Columbiad,* 275–285.

Rodgers, Carolyn. "Black Poetry–Where It's At," in Kochman, *Rappin',* 336–345.

Rohlehr, Gordon. "The Shape of That Hurt," in *Voiceprint: An Anthology of Oral and Related Poetry from the Caribbean,* edited by Stewart Brown, Mervyn Morris, and Gordon Rohlehr. Harlow, U.K.: Longman, 1989. 1–23.

Rose, Tricia. "Rhythmic Repetition, Industrial Forces and Black Practice," In Sexton, *Rap on Rap,* 45–55.

Sanchez, Sonia. "The Poet as a Creator of Social Values." *Black Scholar* 16 (Jan.–Feb. 1985): 20–24.

Scott, Nathan A., Jr. "Black Literature," in Hoffman, *Harvard Guide to Contemporary American Writing,* 287–341.

Smith, David Lionel. "Chicago Poets, OBAC and the Black Arts Movement," in Bercovitch, *Reconstructing American Literary History,* 250–279.

Smith, Gary. "The Literary Ballads of Sterling A. Brown." *CLA Journal* 32 (1989): 393–409.

Sollors, Werner. "A Critique of Pure Pluralism," in Bercovitch, *Reconstructing American Literary History,* 250–279.

Story, Ralph. "Paul Laurence Dunbar: Master Player in a Fixed Game." *CLA Journal* 27 (1978): 30–55.

Tracy, Steven C. " A MELUS Interview: Etheridge Knight." *MELUS* 12, no. 2 (summer 1985): 7–23.

Van Hallsberg, Robert. "American Poet-Critics since 1945," in Bercovitch, *Reconstructing American Literary History,* 280–289.

Ward, Jerry W. "Alvin Aubert: The Levee, the Blues, the Mighty Mississippi." *BALF* 23 (1989): 415–440.

Williams, Sherley Ann. "The Blues Roots of Afro-American Poetry," in Fisher and Stepto, *Afro-American Literature,* 72–87.

RECORDED POETRY

Angelou, Maya. *Poetry.* LP. GWP Records, 1989.

———. *Phenomenal Woman.* Audiocassette. Audiobooks–Random House, 1995.

Anthology of Negro Poets, edited by Arna Bontemps, with readings by Langston Hughes, Sterling Brown, Claude McKay, Countee Cullen, Gwendolyn Brooks, and Margaret Walker. LP. Folkways, 1966.

Baraka, Amiri (LeRoi Jones). *Black and Beautiful Soul and Madness.* LP. Jihad c. 1969.

———. *It's Nation Time: African Visionary Music.* LP. Motown–Black Forum, 1972.

———. *New Music–New Poetry,* with David Murray and Steve McCall. LP. India Navigations, 1981.

———. "Wailers," *Life Is a Killer.* LP. Giorno Poetry Systems, 1982.

Beyond the Blues: American Negro Poetry, edited by Dr. Rosey E. Pool. Read by Brock Peters, Gordon Heath, Vinette Carroll, Cleo Laine. LP. Decca-Argo, c. 1963.

Black Spirits: Festival of New Black Poets in America, with readings by Imamu Amiri Baraka, Kali, Johari Amini, Clarence Major, David Henderson, Norman Jordan, Askia Muhammad Toure, The Original Last Poets, Stanley Crouch, Jackie Earley, Amus Moore, Larry Neal. LP. Motown-Black Forum, 1972.

Brooks, Gwendolyn. *Reading Her Poetry* with an introductory poem by Don L. Lee. LP. Caedmon, 1969.

Burroughs, Margaret T. *What Shall I Tell My Children Who Are Black?* LP. Sound-A-Rama, c. 1970.

Brown, Sterling, and Langston Hughes. Readings, 1954. LP. Folkways, 1967.

Cortez, Jayne. *Celebrations and Solitudes.* LP. Strata-East, 1974.

———. *Everywhere Drums.* LP. Bola, 1990.

————. "I See Chano Pozo," *Life Is A Killer.* LP. Giorno Poetry Systems, 1982.

Giovanni, Nikki. *Cotton Candy on a Rainy Day.* LP. Folkways, 1978.

————. *Like a Ripple on a Pond,* with the New York Community Choir. LP. Atlantic-Niktom, 1973.

————. *Truth Is On Its Way,* with the New York Community Choir. LP. Right-On, c. 1971.

————. *The Way I Feel.* LP. Atlantic-Niktom, 1975.

Hughes, Langston. *The Black Verse: 12 Moods for Jazz.* LP. Buddha, c. 1968.

————. *The Dream Keeper and Other Poems.* LP. Folkways, 1955.

————. *Langston Hughes Reads and Talks about His Poems.* LP. Spoken Arts, 1959.

————. *Poetry and Reflections.* Audiocassette. Caedmon, 1980.

————. *Weary Blues.* LP. MGM-Verve, c. 1958. With music.

————. and Margaret Danner. *Writers of the Revolution.* LP. Motown-Black Forum, 1970.

Kain, Gylan. *The Blue Guerilla.* LP. Juggernaut, c. 1971.

The Language of Life: A Festival of Poets. Hosted for PBS by Bill Moyers. With readings by Sekou Sundiata, Michael S. Harper, Victor Hernandez Cruz, and Lucille Clifton.Audiocassette. BDD Audio-Public Affairs Television, 1995.

The Last Poets. *At Last.* LP. Blue Thumb, c. 1973.

————. *Chastisement.* LP. Blumb Thumb, c. 1972.

————. *Holy Terror.* LP. Rycodisc-Black Arc, 1993.

————. *The Last Poets.* LP. Douglas, c. 1970.

————. *This Is Madness.* LP. Douglas, c. 1970.

Komunyakaa, Yusef, and John Tchicai. *Notes from the Madhouse.* CD. Eighth Harmonic Breakdown, 1998.

Madhubuti, Haki R. (Don L. Lee). *Medasi* with Nation-Afrikan Liberation Art Ensemble. LP. Rise, 1984.

————. *Rappin' and Readin'.* LP. Broadside Voices, c. 1970.

————. *Rise Vision Comin* with the Afrikan Liberation Art Ensemble. LP. Rise, 1976.

The Original Last Poets. *Right On!* From the film starring David Nelson, Felipe Luciano, Gylan Kain. LP. Juggernaut, c. 1969.

Parker, Pat, and Judy Grahn. *Where Would I Be Without You?* LP. Olivia, 1976.

Reed, Ishmael. *Conjure: Cab Calloway Stands in for the Moon.* LP. American Clave, 1988.

————. *Conjure: Music for the Texts of Ishmael Reed.* LP. American Clave-I.R.S., 1984.

Sanchez, Sonia. "Letter to Dr. Martin Luther King, Jr.," performed by Sweet Honey in the Rock, *Live At Carnegie Hall.* LP. EarthBeat, 1988.

————. "Stay on the Battlefied"/"I Have Come to the City," with Sweet Honey in the Rock. *Sacred Ground.* Earth Beat!, 1995.

————. *A Sun Lady for All Seasons Reads Her Poetry.* LP. Folkways, 1971.

Scott-Heron, Gil. *A New Black Poet: Small Talk at 125th and Lenox.* LP. Flying Dutchman, 1970.

Smith, Patricia. *Always in the Head and Selected poems.* Audiocassette. Zoland Books, 1993.

Walker, Alice. *My Life as Myself.* With eight original poems. Audiocassette. Sounds True, 1995.

Yarbrough, Camille. *The Iron Pot Cooker.* Vanguard, 1975.

Copyrights and Permissions

Note: The author has made every attempt to obtain permission for all works quoted in this book by contacting either the authors themselves or their agents and third-party copyright holders. Below is a list of permissions obtained.

"Narrative: Ali Part 12" by Elizabeth Alexander. Copyright © Elizabeth Alexander. Used with permission of the author.

"Black People" "I Am Speaking of Goodness. . ." by Amiri Baraka. Used with permission of the author.

"Winnie," "Martin Luther King Jr.," "Of DeWitt Williams. . .," "The boy died in my alley," "Sermon on the Warpland," "Infirm" from works of Gwendolyn Brooks © by 1991 by Gwendolyn Brooks. Used with permission of the author.

"Crossing," "Glory, Glory" from *The Collected Poems of Sterling A. Brown*, edited by Michael S. Harper; copyright © 1980 by Sterling A. Brown. Reprinted by permission of HarperCollins Publishers, Inc.

"Lately everybody I meet is a poet" and "Harriet" © Lucille Clifton. Reprinted from *Good Woman Poems and a Memoir, 1969–1980* by Lucille Clifton with permission of BOA Editions, Lt., 260 East Avenue, Rochester, NY 14804.

Excerpt of "Doing Battle with the Wolf" by Wanda Coleman. Copyright © 1990 by Wanda Coleman. Reprinted from *African Sleeping Sickness: Stories and Poems* with permission of Black Sparrow Press.

"Aunt Ida Pieces a Quilt" by Melvin Dixon appears in *Love's Instrument* (Tia Chucha Press, 1995) and is reprinted with permission of the Estate of Melvin Dixon and of Dorothy Beam.

"Hoochie Coochie Man" by Willie Dixon © 1957, 1964, 1992 Hoochie Coochie Music, administered by Bug Music. All rights reserved. Used by permission. For more information please contact: The Blues Heaven Foundation, Inc., 2120 S. Michigan Avenue, Chicago, IL 60616.

"Ego-tripping" and "Revolutionary Dreams" copyright © 1968 by Nikki Giovanni, used with permission of the author.

Index

About the Author

Fahamisha Patricia Brown is associate professor of English in the department of languages and literature at Austin Peay State University in Clarksville, Tennessee. Having been introduced to the works of Paul Laurence Dunbar, Langston Hughes, and Gwendolyn Brooks as a young girl, she has read, studied, performed, and taught the works of African American poets for over thirty-five years. Her essays and articles about African American poets and writers have been published in several reference works. She is also coeditor of a tribute volume to Gwendolyn Brooks, *To Gwen, With Love*.